LIVING
FENCES

LIVING FENCES

A GARDENER'S GUIDE TO
Hedges, Vines & Espaliers

OGDEN TANNER

CHAPTERS™

CHAPTERS PUBLISHING LTD., SHELBURNE, VERMONT 05482

Published by
Chapters Publishing Ltd.
2031 Shelburne Road
Shelburne, Vermont 05482

Library of Congress Cataloging-in-Publication Data
Tanner, Ogden.
    Living Fences : a gardener's guide to hedges, vines, and espaliers / by
Ogden Tanner.
        p.   cm.
    Includes bibliographical references (p.) and index.
    ISBN 1-881527-67-0: $29.95.—ISBN 1-881527-68-9: $19.95
    1. Hedges. 2. Ornamental climbing plants. 3. Espaliers. 4. Screens
    (Plants) I. Title.
SB437.T37 1995
635.9'76—dc20   94-25263

Trade distribution by
Firefly Books Ltd.
250 Sparks Avenue
Willowdale, Ontario
Canada M2H 2S4

Printed and bound in Canada by Metropole Litho, Inc.
St. Bruno de Montarville, Quebec

Designed by Susan J. McClellan
Front cover: Photograph by Richard W. Brown

Other books by Ogden Tanner

The New York Botanical Garden: An Illustrated Chronicle

Gardening America

Garden Rooms

Rock and Water Gardens

Herbs

Garden Construction

CONTENTS

PLANTS FOR PRIVACY AND BEAUTY

I S IT TOO MUCH TO EXPECT that a house, the single largest investment that most people will make, be not just a shelter, but an oasis, a place where peace and privacy can be enjoyed at the end of a busy day? Why, then, is it that modern building practices make that serenity nearly impossible to secure?

More often than not, the back yard offers an unwanted view of the neighbors' houses. The hum of tires and the intermittent flashes of headlights from passing traffic on a busy street can disturb the peace in front. Local pets may wander in uninvited from all sides. High stockade fences and masonry walls can provide privacy, but are seldom the answer. They are not only expensive, but are also likely to be resented as unneighborly warnings to "Keep Out!" They may also be illegal under local zoning codes, particularly in front yards, where their ability to block out the street may be most wanted.

The solution is a living fence, a wall of plants that, with branches and foliage, will screen out views and gently, tactfully reinforce boundaries.

While a tall, formal evergreen hedge may come to mind, there are other alternatives. It is a great misconception about hedges to assume that they have to be formal: neatly clipped and rectilinear, with plants in a rigid row, needing to be sheared often in order to maintain their shape.

Far more practical and beautiful solutions can be found among the creative and unexpected use of plants. With a modern ranch house—or even an older Victorian home—an informal, unshaped hedge of shrubs planted in one single or a staggered double row may feel more natural, and will definitely be easier to maintain.

A species chosen for its natural grace of habit, such as yellow-flowered forsythia with its arching stems, will provide year-round screening and joyful spring color while requiring minimal, once-a-year pruning after it flowers to remove broken, diseased or dead canes.

THREE FEET MAY BE ALL THERE IS between your neighbor's property line and the side of your house. While there may seem to be no option but a fence, vines, both annual and perennial, are equally useful as living fences, and can be brought into play without the time, effort and expense involved in planting a hedge. Trained over a trellis or a post-and-wire structure, a fast-growing vine can be used in place of a hedge to block out a view, and will often do so in a single growing season.

Vines can be employed to decorate an expanse of otherwise unadorned wall, whether on the house itself or a windowless garage. They can be trained to brighten up a bland wooden fence or an unattractive chain-link enclosure around a swimming pool. Vines add a new, vertical note to the existing garden, and many are valued for their dense, covering foliage or their stun-

ning displays of flowers. And, unlike hedges, which can spread eight feet or more horizontally, vines will thrive in a narrow planting bed often less than a foot across.

SOMETHING MORE FORMAL, more permanent than a vine, can be had with an espalier. Espaliering makes a host of ordinary garden plants, some generally used in hedges and others as trees, behave, in effect, as if they were vines. From firethorns to apricots, espaliers offer a way to grow plants that the gardener with little space to spare might usually dismiss as requiring too much room. Like vines, espaliers are grown flat against a wall, a trellis or a freestanding structure of posts and wires, and require planting beds smaller than those of the average hedge. And, like vines, they can be used to define an area, obscure an unwanted view or serve as decoration, highlighting a blank or empty space.

Espaliers, however, are not the quick, instant solution to a landscaping problem that vines can be. They grow slowly, and require careful training and pruning. Some patterns may take as long as four years to complete, and must then be pruned to keep the pattern intact. It may seem like too much trouble for too little reward, but an espalier pays back the hard work lavished on it with rich displays of blossoms and fruit—often more plentiful than on a regular, unespaliered plant—and the decorative pattern of its branches, which can be enjoyed in every season, even when the leaves have fallen and the branches are bare.

Espaliers are usually trained into one of the many traditional, formal patterns that have evolved over the years, such as repetitive vertical or diagonal cordons, latticework, or fan- and candelabra-like designs. Another option is to train an espalier informally, relying instead on a plant's natural tendencies, and shaping it in any way the gardener is inspired. Such informal shapes are almost unlimited, depending only on the gardener's ingenuity and the natural beauty of a particular plant.

ALL OF THE LIVING FENCES can do more than screen views or act as property-line boundaries. Hedges, vines and espaliers can also act as partitions to enclose or divide gardens and sitting areas. The division between a vegetable garden and outdoor entertaining area can be defined with a row of bridalwreath spiraea, or a trellis covered with morning glory vines. Apple trees, whose beauty and practicality suit both the workaday vegetable garden and the entertaining area, can be espaliered to a post-and-wire framework. After a few years, the trees will be thick enough to screen the view of the garden while providing useful fruit. A low planting of germander, neatly sheared, can define a planned garden path, keeping pedestrian traffic within bounds and away from areas of the yard that are used for more mundane purposes, such as composting.

A smaller living fence can hide an outdoor work space from the rest of the garden, so that tools and other equipment are stored out of sight. A short row of a few shrubs will do the trick. If you must have a fence, train an annual vine like bittersweet to it as camouflage. Or make an informal, fan-shaped espalier with one of the many viburnums available. It will provide not only lush green foliage but also springtime flowers, autumn berries and bright color, and a wintertime enjoyment of the pattern revealed underneath.

There is a living fence of some kind or another for you, whatever your screening or camouflage needs might be. This book offers suggestions and ideas, but it is up to you, the gardener, to determine what is most appropriate. Good choosing—and good luck!

CHAPTER ONE

HEDGES
FORMAL & INFORMAL

HE WORD "HEDGE" MAKES MANY GARDENERS think of a tall, dark and rigidly formal border of ever-greens—a labor-intensive replacement for a high fence, demanding constant shearing in order to maintain its squared-off shape. Hedges, however, can be much more than living property-line markers. In fact, there are as many possible kinds of hedges as there are shrub and tree species and individual gardeners with problem landscapes.

A hedge need not be tall. Korean littleleaf boxwood or germander, which grow to only about 1½ feet high, make ideal borders for a path or a flower bed. Hedges need not be evergreen. Tall, mature roses, firethorns and five-leaf aralias can act as barriers to keep dogs, children and others within bounds. Shrubs like Alpine currant or compact American cranberrybush, which grow about 5 feet high, can be arranged in attractive groupings to enclose a terrace or to create a welcoming entrance garden between the front door and a busy street. A short row of summersweet or flowering quince can be planted to obscure the unsightly back wall of a garage or to hide a messy area devoted to children's play.

W HILE HIGHER PLANTINGS CAN edit out unwanted views, they can also serve as dark, stunning back-drops for garden flowers. A staggered row of evergreens like hemlocks, arranged near the lot line, can not only provide privacy but also help absorb street noise, mitigate pollution from automobiles and break a chilling winter wind. Five or six white pines, arranged in a circle toward the back of a lot, can make an ideal "secret" enclosure for a children's sandbox, or a table and chairs. Inside, you'll feel far away from everything, deep in piney woods.

Although used to accomplish the same ends, hedges have a definite advantage over fences and walls. As part of a living landscape, a well-planted hedge will seem to belong to its setting. Hedges are also more neighborly, defining spaces politely without need for the harsh presence of fences or walls.

Personally, I prefer the informal kind of hedge, one that can be left to grow naturally, and whose blossoms and berries will attract birds, butterflies and bees. Honeysuckles, for exam-ple, make a fine low-maintenance hedge. Their attractive and often fragrant flowers come in a variety of colors—pink, white, red or yellow. Their red or yellow berries, which are relished by birds, are another bonus.

Bear in mind, however, that an informal hedge can take up a great deal of ground space, even growing twice as wide as it is tall. Be particularly careful when locating one near a property line. It can soon outgrow its allotted space and start encroaching on a neighbor's property, leaving the embarrassing task of shear-ing it back. In fact, it is a good idea to discuss any property-line hedge or windbreak with the person next door. Good hedges, like good fences, make good neighbors.

Right: Mixed evergreens make a striking back-drop and screen. Previous page: A low, trimmed border of germander defines a garden path.

An informal hedge of a deciduous species, planted in a staggered double or a single row, can provide all the screening benefits of a formal, evergreen hedge without the careful pruning needed to maintain it. Above: Euonymous alata (winged burning bush) is a graceful plant whose leaves turn a vibrant red color in the fall, making it a winning choice for such informal hedges.

In planning a hedge, first consider what you want it to do. Is it to enclose a garden without cutting it off from the outside world? Is it to shield a row of trash containers from view? Is it to define a property line? To act as a windbreak? To keep dogs and children from taking shortcuts?

For edging a garden bed, you may want nothing more than a low line of boxwood, perhaps 18 inches high, that can be neatly sheared. Or lavender, which will provide a sweet-smelling edging that requires almost no shaping. For hiding the trash cans, consider a short row of evergreen shrubs such as holly, allowed to grow informally to 4 feet. If you prefer flowers, however, perhaps glossy abelia is a possibility. A substantial planting of white pine or hemlock, arranged in a line or in staggered rows, may be what you need to screen the neighbors or disperse a biting winter wind. If you need to deter wandering feet, a hedge of thorny, densely branched barberry will do the trick, while pleasing the eye in all seasons. Its bright red berries will hang on to provide cheerful color in winter after the leaves have fallen.

CHOOSING A HEDGE

IN CHOOSING A PLANT FOR A HEDGE, you should bear in mind several factors: how fast it grows, how large it can get and whether it is deciduous or will remain evergreen year round. Other things to consider are the size and shape of leaves, the color and timing of flowers and berries and whether the foliage will turn an attractive color in the fall. If young children will be around your hedge, be aware of the plants that can be toxic. While children should be discouraged from eating any ornamental planting, you may want to avoid a crisis by steering away from very poisonous shrubs.

Equally important in considering your hedge is whether or not the plant will grow in the area in which you live, whether it needs full sun or can stand partial shade, and whether it has special requirements regarding soil. It is a good idea to look around your neighborhood to see what kinds of hedge plants are in use, and to ask their owners how they are doing under local conditions. For specific information about the plant's general attributes, such as height, fruit and flower colors and whether or not it is poisonous, see the species descriptions in this chapter, and the Zone Map on pages 120-121.

Since buying enough plants for a sizable hedge can be fairly expensive, often running to many hundreds of dollars, it is critical that you do it correctly. Beware of "bargains" at garden centers and discount stores. Go to a reputable nursery, where you are much more likely to find a salesperson who is also a professional horticulturist, and where plants are apt to be grown locally, and thus are accustomed to local conditions, rather than shipped in from hundreds of miles away.

If possible, go to nurseries on a weekday or an off-season weekend rather than on a busy spring Saturday; the nursery staff will be less frantic and have more time to attend to your needs. Some nurseries will be happy to send an expert to your house to guide you in choosing plants. And, of course, most nurseries will do the planting for you—for a fee—and will guarantee, for a period of time, the future health of the plants that they put in place. In any case, don't forget to ask about quantity discounts, which many nurseries offer for larger orders.

THE THREE FORMS OF PLANTS SOLD BY NURSERIES

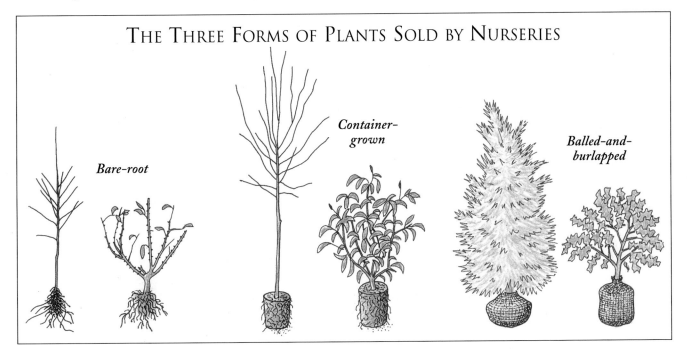

Bare-root

Container-grown

Balled-and-burlapped

WHEN YOU DECIDE ON A SPECIES, ask the salesperson to set the plants out in a row so you can examine them for bushiness and uniformity of growth. Evergreen hedge plants in particular should be branched down to the ground; deciduous ones, which will be cut back drastically after planting, should have healthy root balls and good top growth. The more buds there are on the branches, the better.

Reject any plants that are spindly or have an excessive amount of dead or broken branches or shriveled bark. Pass up any with wilted or brownish leaves or leaves that are smaller than normal for the species, indications that the root systems are poor or that the plants have been inadequately watered.

Look for a healthy green color; a yellowish or mottled appearance is suspect. Also look at leaves for discolored spots that suggest fungus disease, and holes that indicate insects have been feeding on them. Check the joints where the leaves are attached to the stems for colonies of mealy bugs, which resemble soft white cotton. Examine the plant for spider mites by holding a piece of paper under the leaves and shaking them to see if tiny, dancing dots appear. Check the stems for cankers, which look like dark knots; they will eventually cut off the flow of sap, killing the plant unless the afflicted stems are cut off.

Do not be tempted to buy big, mature shrubs to create an instant effect. They are not only more expensive than younger ones, but may suffer shock during transplanting unless carefully dug up from their nursery beds and moved. Instead, buy younger plants, about half the size they will be when full grown. For example, if a shrub can be expected to reach 6 feet tall at maturity, get a 3-foot specimen. If the species is of the spreading type, the key dimension will be its diameter: a shrub expected to spread 6 feet should be purchased when it is no more than 3 feet wide.

Plants are generally offered in three forms.

The cheapest—and the one favored by mail-order nurseries because of its ease of shipping—is bare-rooted, that is, shipped when the plants are leafless and dormant and with their roots free of soil. Good nurseries and mail-order houses pack the roots in dampened moss and plastic to keep them moist. If you cannot plant right away, store them out of the sun in a carport or unheated garage. Do not allow them to dry out, or the plants will die.

Bare-rooted transplanting limits the selling season to when the plants are dormant, which generally means planting them in early spring (or winter in milder climates). For this reason most local nurseries offer plants balled-and-burlapped or growing in containers, so that they can be planted at any time of the year that the ground can be worked.

A container-grown plant is a plant whose root ball is contained in a plastic or metal pot. A balled-and-burlapped plant is one whose soil ball, roots and all, has been dug out of the ground, wrapped in burlap and tied up with twine. Both cost more than bare-rooted plants because of the time and labor involved in growing and preparing them. But they can be planted over a long period, and since they go into the ground with roots surrounded by the soil in which they have been growing, they suffer little transplanting shock.

PLANTING A HEDGE

SPRING IS THE BEST TIME TO plant most species; a shrub planted then has months to establish itself before winter arrives. Many, however, can also be planted in fall, when the soil is drier and hence easier to work. The soil then is also warm enough so that new roots will sprout even though the shrub has ceased summer growth; the following spring, these roots will give the plant a head start over shrubs planted at winter's end. Fall is also when nurseries often offer price reductions in order

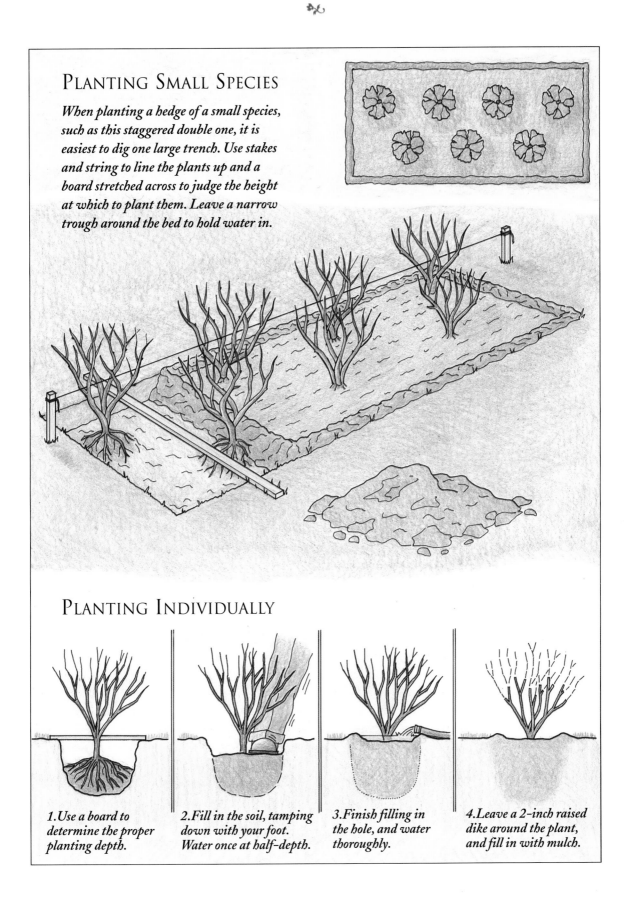

PLANTING SMALL SPECIES

When planting a hedge of a small species, such as this staggered double one, it is easiest to dig one large trench. Use stakes and string to line the plants up and a board stretched across to judge the height at which to plant them. Leave a narrow trough around the bed to hold water in.

PLANTING INDIVIDUALLY

1. Use a board to determine the proper planting depth.

2. Fill in the soil, tamping down with your foot. Water once at half-depth.

3. Finish filling in the hole, and water thoroughly.

4. Leave a 2-inch raised dike around the plant, and fill in with mulch.

to get rid of their inventory before winter sets in, and true bargains can sometimes be had at this time. If you suffer from cold winters, however, it is best to plant in the spring, when the danger of frost is past. A fall-planted shrub's new growth may be killed by winter's onset.

It is a good idea to test the pH of your soil before planting, either with a simple kit sold at garden centers or, more reliably, by sending soil samples to a state or county agricultural extension agent. Most hedge plants will do well in a soil that is mildly acid, registering between 6.0 and 7.0. Some plants, like laurel and summersweet, like a more acid reading of 4.5 to 5.5. To lower the pH ½ to 1 unit, apply 3 pounds of iron sulfate to each 100 square feet of soil (since it drains away, you may need to replace it every two or three years by sprinkling the powder on the ground and watering it into the soil). For soils that are too acid for the species you want to grow, add finely ground dolomitic limestone to the soil at a rate of 5 pounds per 100 square feet. Since limestone is slow-acting, apply it several months ahead of time. For a spring planting, mix it into the soil in the fall so that it has all winter to soak in.

LARGER SCREENING PLANTS like white pine and hemlock can be planted some distance apart in individual holes. For each, dig a hole that is twice the diameter of the root ball and one and a half times its depth. As you dig, make separate piles of the darker topsoil and the lighter subsoil. To improve drainage and moisture retention, and to admit the air needed for good root growth, mix 1 part peat moss, compost or leaf mold to 2 parts of soil in each pile.

Then start filling in the hole with the rich topsoil mix, which will give the roots nourishment. You can add a couple of handfuls of slow-acting, non-burning fertilizer such as bone meal or cottonseed meal, digging it into the bottom of the hole and around the roots. Try setting the plant in the hole; it should be planted at the same level as it was in the nursery. Continue to fill around the root ball with more topsoil mix until the hole is three-quarters full. Tamp down the earth with your foot and fill the remaining space with water.

When the water has drained off, fill the hole completely with the remaining subsoil mix and make a "saucer"—a circular dike of soil about 2 inches high—around the perimeter. Then water thoroughly again. To retain moisture and keep down weeds, apply a 2-inch mulch of ground bark or wood chips, or a 3-to-4-inch mulch of compressible materials like leaf mold or pine needles.

FOR MOST SMALLER SPECIES, it is simpler to dig a long trench with a rototiller, if you have or can rent or borrow one. For a single row of plants, this trench should be one and one half times as deep as the root balls and at least a foot wider, so that the plants will have 6 inches of prepared soil on each side. For a staggered, double row of plants, make the trench proportionately wider. Depending on the species, plants should generally be set from 1 to 3 feet apart.

If there is grass growing over the area where you plan to make your trench, cut the sod with a shovel and turn it upside down in the bottom of the trench when you have finished digging; it will decompose to provide nutrients for the hedge plants' roots. Mix the soil with a generous amount of peat moss, leaf mold or compost to improve drainage and retain moisture. A light dusting of bone meal or dried cow manure will give slow-growing species a boost.

Bare-root plants should not be allowed to dry out, and they should have their roots soaking in water for an hour or so before being planted. Set a bare-root plant in the trench atop a mound of topsoil enriched with organic matter, adjusting the plant to the height at which it was previously growing (a board laid across the trench will help you gauge this). Spread the roots out and over the mound of soil, and fill in

CONTAINER-GROWN PLANTS

Water a container-grown plant before removing
it from the pot. Use a ruler to judge the depth
at which it will be planted.

Open the container gently and loosen
the tight, pot-bound roots.

Use a board to gauge the height.
Then fill the hole with soil, leaving a
2-inch dike around the plant. Water
thoroughly and mulch to
conserve moisture.

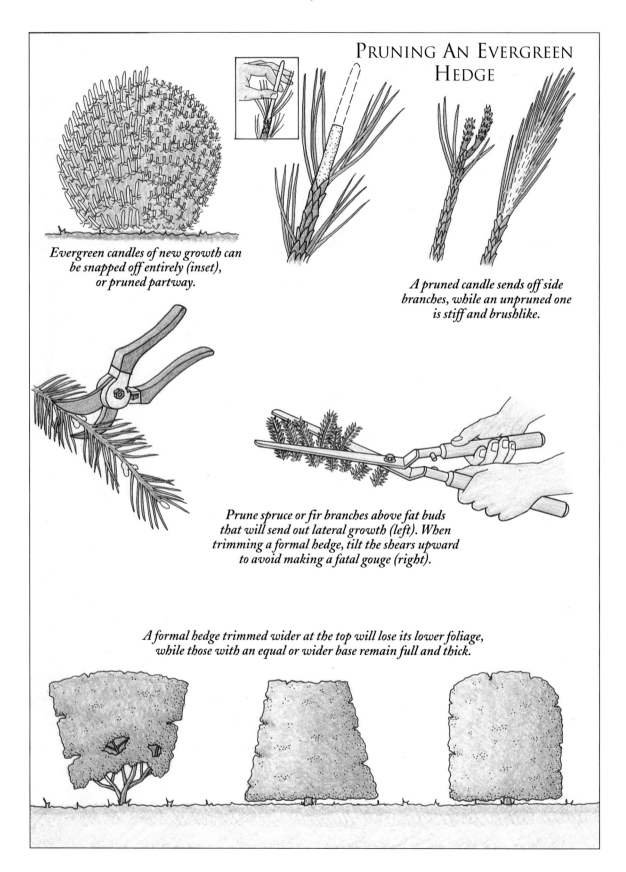

PRUNING AN EVERGREEN
HEDGE

*Evergreen candles of new growth can
be snapped off entirely (inset),
or pruned partway.*

*A pruned candle sends off side
branches, while an unpruned one
is stiff and brushlike.*

*Prune spruce or fir branches above fat buds
that will send out lateral growth (left). When
trimming a formal hedge, tilt the shears upward
to avoid making a fatal gouge (right).*

*A formal hedge trimmed wider at the top will lose its lower foliage,
while those with an equal or wider base remain full and thick.*

until the hole is three-quarters full, repeating this procedure with the rest of the plants. Stretch a string on stakes above the trench as a guideline to make sure the plants are lined up correctly with each other, either in a single straight row or a double, staggered row. Water the plants thoroughly, then fill in the rest of the soil, tamping lightly around the plants with your foot. Leave a narrow trough around the edges of the trench to hold water and define the planting bed. Then water again.

Container-grown plants should be watered before their pots are removed. Inspect them for matted roots, which sometimes wind around in a futile search for new soil. Gently pry the outer roots apart, trying to break as few as possible, and spread them out before planting. Balled-and-burlapped plants can be placed directly in the trench, and the top of the burlap loosened and cut away. (If the burlap has been treated to retard rotting or the wrapping is made of non-biodegradable material—ask the nursery—remove it before planting.) After planting is completed, mulch the top of the plant bed with 2 or 3 inches of ground bark or leaf mold to hold in moisture, keep soil temperatures even and suppress the growth of weeds.

PRUNING HEDGES

PRUNE THE PLANTS AS SOON as they are in the ground, if the nursery has not already done so. Bare-root shrubs are usually pruned after being pulled from their holding bed—otherwise, their branches would overwhelm the roots remaining.

For deciduous plants that will become an informal hedge, take off about a third of the top growth, including any overly long or badly placed branches. Do not cut all the stems to an even height. Maintain the shrub's natural shape by removing a proportional amount from the top of each stem. Make each cut about ¼ inch above an outward-facing bud. Then allow the plants to grow for a full season before pruning again.

For a formal hedge, deciduous plants that are not bushy down to their bases should be cut back drastically—to within 4 or 5 inches of the ground. Though it might seem that one would kill the plants with such treatment, the stubs will actually sprout two to six new stems for every old one; within a few months, the plants will be as tall as they were originally—and far denser and bushier. If you lose heart and make the cut at 12 inches above the ground, the thick new growth will start from there, and the bottom foot of the shrubs will remain forever bare. Prune evergreen plants, whether for a formal or informal hedge, very lightly, and leave them to grow for a full season.

TO GET THEM OFF TO A PROPER START, new hedges should be watered about once every week or 10 days during the growing season, less if there are heavy rains. For proper root growth, it is important to water deeply or not at all. Rather than stand around sprinkling by hand, invest in a canvas soaker hose, which delivers water slowly, allowing it to penetrate the root zone without runoff.

The following spring you can begin shaping a formal hedge. A cardinal rule here is: *keep the bottom wider than the top.* This would seem to go against the natural growth of most plants, which tends to be wider at the top than at the bottom. But it is essential that the leaves at the bottom get sunlight, and the sloping sides will allow just that. If you do not shape the hedge to permit this, the lower branches will be constantly shaded and will die, leaving the lower part of the hedge bare.

The top of the hedge, as long as it is narrower than the bottom, can be either rounded or flat. In northern areas, a rounded shape is preferable for shedding heavy accumulations of snow, which on a flat top can add so much weight that the branches may break or be forced apart.

A formal hedge needs shearing when new

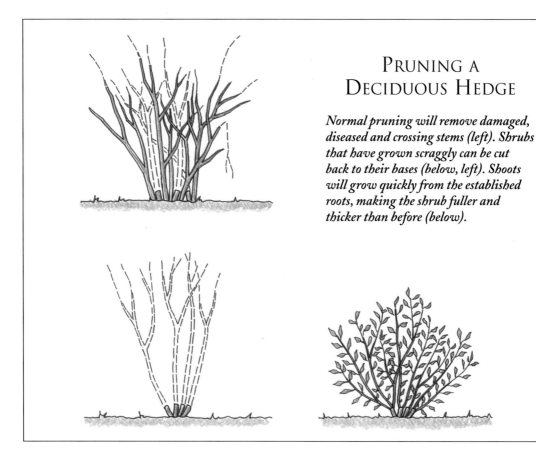

PRUNING A DECIDUOUS HEDGE

Normal pruning will remove damaged, diseased and crossing stems (left). Shrubs that have grown scraggly can be cut back to their bases (below, left). Shoots will grow quickly from the established roots, making the shrub fuller and thicker than before (below).

growth becomes about 6 inches long. Regular trimming will induce each clipped stem to produce several twigs, making for a thicker, healthier hedge. In colder climates—Zone 6 and northward—try not to shear after midsummer, as new growth should have time to "harden" before the arrival of winter.

As a guide to shearing the top, stretch a string between stakes embedded in the ground, using a carpenter's level to make sure the string is in line. You can use manual hedge shears or electrically powered shears. Be especially careful with the latter, however, as a slip of the hand will leave a gouge that will take a lot of growth to efface. When using electric shears, follow the manufacturer's safety instructions. Do not wear loose clothing or dangling jewelry, which can be caught in moving parts. Use gloves, safety glasses and non-skid footwear, keep both hands on the handles provided and don't try to cut stems more than ⅜ inch thick.

MUCH OF THE CHARM of informal hedges comes from the flowers and fruits they produce, so it is important to prune them for maximum bloom. Before you do any pruning, make sure you know the growth habits of your particular plants. Shrubs such as forsythias and flowering quinces blossom from buds formed on stems that grew during the previous summer. They should be pruned after they have flowered and before buds start to form on the current year's growth. Other shrubs, such as roses of Sharon, bloom from buds formed on the current season's growth. They should be pruned in early spring before new growth starts, just as the buds that will produce new stems begin to swell. Pruning them then will encourage each stem to put out several strong, flowering shoots.

Deciduous hedges that have become old, long-legged or otherwise overgrown can be renewed by cutting the whole hedge back to

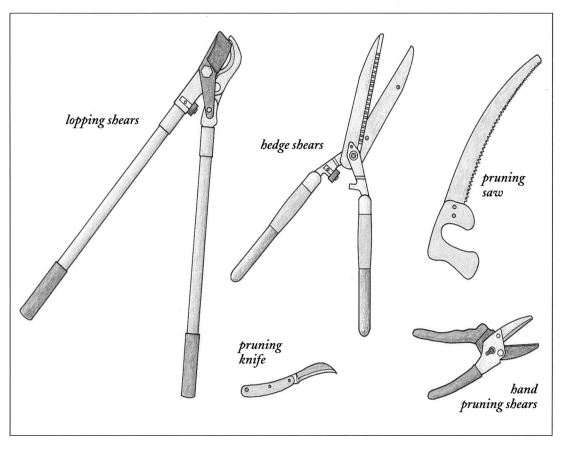

lopping shears

hedge shears

pruning saw

pruning knife

hand pruning shears

within 4 or 5 inches of the ground. Although this may seem to defeat the purpose of a thick, leafy hedge, the mature roots will send out new shoots and the plant will grow back thicker than before. Do such pruning in early spring, when the sap is stirring. An application of general-purpose fertilizer or bone meal, scratched into the soil around the base of the plants, will make new growth appear faster.

PRUNING HEDGES IS NOT DIFFICULT. First, look for dead, damaged or diseased branches, and remove them at any time to maintain the health of the plants. Second, bear in mind that you can steer the plant's growth by choosing where you cut a healthy branch. If you cut ¼ inch above an outward-facing leaf bud, it will produce a new branch that grows outward, opening up the center of the plant and increasing its spread. If you cut ¼ inch above an inward-facing leaf bud, it will produce a branch that grows inward, making the shrub denser—a good way to thicken up a plant that is growing open and scraggly. Make the cut at a 45-degree angle and just enough above the bud so you do not either damage it or leave a long stub.

A pair of ordinary pruning shears—either a scissors type or a blade-and-anvil type—will work on stems up to about half an inch in diameter. For stems any larger, use a pair of lopping shears, whose long handles will give you the added leverage necessary (some have gears or levers that increase the amount of force you can bring to bear). For branches too large for loppers—which you may encounter in cutting back a shrub to the ground to revitalize it—you may need a pruning saw. Its teeth are more widely angled than those of a carpenter's saw to keep them from binding in sap-filled wood, and it generally cuts on the pulling stroke rather than the pushing one. Use tools of good quality and

Right: Layering deciduous and evergreen plants creates the illusion of stillness and quiet in a busy garden. Overleaf: A hedge of European beech blocks out the outside world, forming a solid backdrop for a widely-spaced row of cypresses.

keep them cleaned, oiled and sharp. If you have to use one on diseased wood, clean the cutting surfaces with denatured alcohol before reusing.

REMEMBER, DO ANY SUBSTANTIAL pruning of spring-flowering deciduous shrubs right after the flowers fade, so that the plant's energy can immediately go into producing new growth and flower buds for the following year. With summer-flowering plants, it is better to wait until the next spring to remove old stems. Fall pruning can stimulate tender new growth that will be subject to killing frosts, and can rob a shrub of decorative berries. With flowering evergreen shrubs, the best time to prune is after flowering.

Pruning evergreens should be done with restraint. First of all, never cut them back to leafless wood, on which these plants cannot produce new buds. For pines and firs, which produce new shoots or "candles" in spring, prune by removing the top half of each partly formed candle, which will result in bushier growth. For hemlocks, junipers and yews, which grow all spring and summer, prune at any time during the growing season by reaching in and lopping just above a side branch so that foliage around it will conceal the cut.

To restrict the growth of evergreens even more effectively, you can root-prune the plants. In spring, just as new buds begin to swell, sink a nurseryman's spade—the kind with a long, flat blade and a square edge—into the ground just below the perimeter of the branches to sever the tips of the roots. You don't have to cut all the roots; sinking the spade at intervals around the perimeter will usually suffice. The plants will grow, but at a slower rate than normal.

SELECTED SPECIES FOR HEDGES
DECIDUOUS

Acanthopanax sieboldianus
(five-leaf aralia)
Informal or formal hedge.
Height: 3 to 6 feet.
Sun or light shade.
Most soils.
Zones 4-9.
Features: Dense, upright, thorny branches make an effective barrier. The leaves hold their color until late autumn, when they turn yellow before dropping. Fast-growing and pest-free, five-leaf aralia tolerates compacted soil and polluted air.
Planting and care: Plant 18 inches to 3 feet apart. Clip at least once a year, or more to maintain a formal hedge. If plants become too tall or gawky, cut them to within a few inches of the ground in early spring; many fresh shoots will quickly appear.

Acer campestre
(hedge maple)
Informal or formal hedge.
Height to 20 feet.
Sun or light shade.
Most soils.
Zones 5-8.
Features: A classic English hedgerow plant, hedge maple has a densely branched globular shape that requires practically no pruning. It is often planted along city streets because it tolerates automobile exhaust fumes.
Planting and care: Plant 3 to 6 feet apart. Hedge maple can be maintained at 4 to 6 feet by pruning.

Acer ginnala
(Amur maple)
Informal hedge.
Height 4 to 15 feet.
Sun or light shade.
Most soils.
Zones 2-8.
Features: A tough, vigorous hedge plant, with small, fragrant white flowers, red winged seed pairs and yellow to orange-red foliage in fall.
Varieties: 'Durand Dwarf' and 'Compactum' are shorter and wider than the species, and make fine, dense hedges 4 to 7 feet tall.
Planting and care: Plant 2 to 4 feet apart for a hedge, up to 8 feet apart for a higher screen. For a leafy base, prune to within a few inches of the ground immediately after planting.

Artemisia abrotanum
(southernwood)
Informal hedge or border.
Height 3 to 5 feet.
Sun or partial shade.
Well-drained soil.
Zones 5-10.
Features: Artemisia's feathery silver-gray foliage, growing in mounds, makes an attractive and drought-tolerant border or hedge for a garden.
Varieties: *A. albula* 'Silver King' is highly recommended.

Planting and care: Plant 1 to 1½ feet apart. Requires little water after plants are established. Pinch the tips to shape.

Berberis spp.
(barberry)
Informal or formal hedge.
Height 4 to 7 feet.
Sun or partial shade.
Most soils.
Zones 5-9.
Features: The arching branches, dense foliage and spines of barberries make them attractive and effective barriers. Most have red-orange foliage in fall. While all barberries carry inedible berries, none are poisonous.
Varieties: Several varieties of deciduous barberries make fine hedges. *B. koreana* (Korean barberry) grows 4 to 6 feet tall and bears both its tiny flowers and

Berberis spp.

Chaenomeles speciosa (flowering quince) *and Forsythia* x *intermedia* (border forsythia)

inedible red berries in clusters. *B. x mentorensis* (Mentor barberry) grows 5 to 7 feet tall and is semi-evergreen, holding its spiny leaves through the year in Zone 7 south but dropping them in colder areas late in fall. *B. thunbergii* (Japanese barberry) grows 4 to 7 feet tall and has bright red and yellow flowers followed by red oval berries. *B. thunbergii* 'Erecta' (truehedge columnberry) has upright rather than arching branches, making it a good choice for a narrower hedge.

Planting and care: Set plants 1 to 3 feet apart. If grown as formal hedges, they may need shearing two or three times a year. If grown informally, little pruning is required. Straggly plants can be cut to within a few inches of the ground and will soon send up new shoots.

Chaenomeles speciosa (flowering quince)
Informal hedge.
Height 4 to 6 feet.
Sun.

Most soils.
Zones 4-8.
Features: Spectacular displays of early-spring flowers—white, pink, orange or red—are followed by shiny red leaves, which turn a deep green in summer. Crowded branches and thorns make a good barrier.
Varieties: Cultivars include 'Nivalis' and 'Snow' (white flowers), 'Phyllis Moore' and 'Gaujardii' (deep pink), 'Apple Blossom' and 'Marmorata' (pink and white), 'Rubra Grandiflora'

and 'Cardinalis' (red).

Planting and care: Buy plants in bloom to make sure of flower color. Plant 2½ to 4 feet apart. To keep a hedge at 3 to 4 feet, prune at least once a year. Cut back an overgrown hedge to within a few inches of the ground. It will soon sprout new branches.

Clethra alnifolia
(summersweet, sweet pepper bush)
Informal hedge.
Height: 4 to 8 feet.
Sun or shade.
Moist, acid soil.
Zones 4-9.
Features: This plant is noted for its deliciously fragrant white or pink flowers, which cover it in the summer. In the fall, summersweet's shiny leaves turn orange in sun to yellow in shade.
Varieties: 'Rosea' has large pale pink flowers. 'Hummingbird' is a low variety, growing about 2 feet tall (it won a 1994 Pennsylvania Horticultural Society Gold Medal Plant Award).
Planting and care: Plant 2 feet apart in soil well mixed with organic matter. Fertilize to promote growth. Prune after flowering.

Cornus mas
(cornelian cherry)
Informal or formal hedge.
Height 4 to 15 feet.
Sun to partial shade.
Most soils.
Zones 4-8.
Features: Small yellow flowers in early spring are followed by ¾-

inch cherrylike fruit, which can be made into tasty preserves. The leaves can be sheared to make a formal hedge. In autumn they turn a dramatic red.
Planting and care: Plant 1 to 2 feet apart for a formal hedge, 2 to 4 feet apart for an informal hedge. Cut back sharply immediately after planting. Fertilize to stimulate slow growth. Informal hedges can be pruned as needed after flowering; formal ones should be sheared in late spring and again in summer.

Cornus racemosa
(gray dogwood)
Informal hedge.
Height 3 to 8 feet.
Sun or shade.
Most soils.
Zones 4-9.
Features: A plant with interest in all seasons: white flowers in late spring, green summer foliage turning purple or red in fall, upright red and gray stems in winter. Tolerates wet ground.
Planting and care: Plant 2 to 3 feet apart. Clip once a year for a neat, informal hedge. Older hedges can be renewed by cutting them back close to the ground.

Cornus sericea
(red osier dogwood)
Informal hedge.
Height 4 to 8 feet.
Sun to partial shade.
Moist soil.
Zones 2-9.
Features: The shrub has creamy white flowers in spring, with red or purple fall foliage. Most out-

standing are the red stems that persist through the winter.
Varieties: *C. sericea kelseyi*, the Kelsey dogwood, has bright red stems that rarely exceed 2 feet in height. *C. sericea flaviramea*, the yellow-twigged dogwood, has new stems that are bright yellow.
Planting and care: Plant 2 to 4 feet apart. Since the color is most intense on younger stems, renew the hedge by cutting it back to the ground every two or three years.

Cotoneaster lucidus
(hedge cotoneaster)
Informal or formal hedge.
Height: 5 to 15 feet.
Sun to shade.
Most soils.
Zones 3-9.
Features: Small, glossy, green leaves crowded on upward-arching stems make this a popular hedge. Foliage turns yellow, orange or red in fall.
Planting and care: Plant 2 to 3 feet apart. Since plants grow rapidly, a formal hedge may need shearing two or three times a year. To renew old hedges, cut them to within a few inches of the ground.

Crataegus crus-galli
(cockspur hawthorn)
Informal hedge.
Height to 30 feet.
Full sun.
Most soils, except wet.
Zones 4-8.
Features: Dark green leaves, 2-inch thorns, and wild branching patterns make this species an impenetrable barrier. White

Fagus sylvatica (European beech)

flowers in late spring are followed by inedible red fruits and fall color that varies from maroon to orange. Cockspur hawthorn tolerates drought, pollution and windy sites.

Varieties: *C. monogyna* 'Inermis' is a thornless cultivar.

Planting and care: Plant 3 to 4 feet apart. Cut back one third, mulch and fertilize to encourage growth. Allow a year to get established, then hand-prune carefully, making sure to preserve the fatter buds that will produce flowers and fruits.

Elaeagnus angustifolia
(Russian olive)
Informal hedge.
Height to 15 feet.
Full sun.
Most soils.
Zones 2-9.

Features: One of the few hedge plants with gray leaves, this species has silvery foliage and bears tiny, yellow, delightfully fragrant flowers in early summer. Tolerant of windy and salty loca-tions, this is a good urban plant.

Planting and care: Plant 3 to 4 feet apart and cut back sharply right after planting. Prune two or three times a year.

Euonymus alata
(winged euonymus, burning bush)
Informal or formal hedge.
Height 3 to 10 feet.
Sun or partial shade.
Most soils.
Zones 3-9.

Features: Named for the winglike ridges that line its stems, the species and its cultivar, *Euonymus alata* 'Compacta' (dwarf burning bush) make fine hedge plants. Most notable is their fall color: an intense pink for the species, a spectacular red for the cultivar when grown in full sun.

Planting and care: Plant the dwarf variety about 2 feet apart, the species about 3 feet apart. Fertilize young plants to bring them to a useful size faster. For a formal hedge, shear once or more a year; for an informal one, clip every other year.

Fagus sylvatica

(European beech)
Formal or informal hedge.
Height to 20 feet or more.
Sun or shade.
Slightly acid, well-drained soil.
Zones 5-10.

Features: Slow-growing, long-lived European beeches can reach 70 feet tall and almost as wide, but can be maintained as hedges as low as 6 feet. They are in fact one of the classic hedge plants of Europe, used for hedgerows in England and as tall hedges on estates. The leaves turn golden bronze in fall, often clinging to the hedge until late winter.

Varieties: 'Atropunicea', sometimes called 'Purpurea', is the famous copper beech, with bronzy green to purplish leaves. 'Riversii' is a dark purple variety sold as Rivers purple beech. 'Asplenifolia' has green, fern-like foliage. 'Fastigiata' is excellent for screening in narrow spaces.

Planting and care: Plant 2 to 4 feet apart for a sheared hedge, 4 to 10 feet apart for a tall screen. Prune in summer or fall; beeches may "bleed" if cut in winter or spring.

Forsythia x *intermedia*

(border forsythia)
Informal hedge.
Height 3 to 8 feet.
Full sun.
Most soils.
Zones 4-9.

Features: Forsythia is used primarily for its spectacular display in early spring, when the arching stems are loaded with bright yellow flowers.

Varieties: 'Spring Glory' has pale yellow flowers; 'Spectabilis' has golden yellow flowers. 'Beatrix Farrand' has large golden blossoms with orange throats and grows to 10 feet high. 'Arnold Dwarf' grows only 2 feet tall but spreads 4 feet wide and bears few flowers; it makes a good low, compact hedge in cold areas.

Planting and care: Plant 2 to 4 feet apart. To preserve the plants' natural grace, and to stimulate the next year's display, prune once a year after flowering.

Hibiscus syriacus

(rose of Sharon, shrub althea)
Informal hedge.
Height 6 to 12 feet.
Sun or partial shade.
Moist, well-drained soil.
Zones 5-9.

Features: Rose of Sharon puts on a show of large, 2½-to-4-inch blossoms in late summer and early fall, long after most shrubs have finished flowering. Its branches are stiffly upright when young but spread with age if not pruned back.

Varieties: 'Diana' has pure white flowers. 'Blue Bird' has light blue blossoms with red throats. 'Woodbridge' has deep rose flowers with red centers. 'Lady Baltimore' has pink flowers with red throats. 'Collie Mullens' has

Hibiscus syriacus
(rose of Sharon)

lavender blooms. 'Double Red' has double red flowers.

Planting and care: Plant 2 to 3 feet apart for a hedge, 3 to 6 feet apart for a taller screen. Roses of Sharon send out leaves very late in spring and bear flowers on the current season's growth. Cut back in winter or early spring to remove crowded branches. Do not shear, as this interferes with flower production. For larger but fewer flowers, cut back each stem to two buds in early spring.

Ilex verticillata (winterberry)

Ilex verticillata
(winterberry)
Informal hedge.
Height 3 to 8 feet.
Sun or light shade.
Moist, acid soils.
Zones 3-8.
Features: The inedible bright red berries show off well against its dark green leaves and smooth gray stems. A good choice for wet places.
Varieties: A dwarf cultivar named 'Nana' is ideal for low hedges and bears larger fruits.

Planting and care: Plant about 4 feet apart. Make sure there is a male plant every six plants or so to ensure berry production.

Lavandula
(lavender)
Informal border.
Height 8 inches to 4 feet.
Full sun or part shade.
Most soils.
Zones 5-10.
Features: A favorite border plant for edging flower beds or pathways, lavender is used for its

gray-green leaves and fragrant flowers, which bloom in spikes and attract bees. It is easy to maintain and tolerant of drought.
Varieties: *L. angustifolia* (English lavender) grows 3 to 4 feet high, *L. dentata* (French lavender) 3 feet high; both have lavender-colored flowers. Some cultivars of *L. angustifolia* are 'Compacta', which reaches only 8 inches and 'Munstead', which tops out at 18 inches. 'Hidcote' grows to 1 foot and has dark blue flowers. 'Jean Davis' reaches 15 inches and has

pale pink flowers that fade to white in summer heat.

Planting and care: Plant 6 inches to 2 feet apart depending on the variety. Remove spent flowers and shear the plants occasionally to keep them neat.

Ligustrum amurense
(Amur privet)
Formal or informal hedge.
Height 3 to 10 feet.
Sun or partial shade.
Most soils.
Zones 4-9.

Features: The classic privet hedge, with small, shiny, dark green leaves. Inexpensive and fast-growing, it tolerates polluted air and compacted soil.

Varieties: *Ligustrum* x *ibolium* (ibolium privet) has been bred for cold-resistance and is the best type commonly available.

Planting and care: Plant 1 to 2 feet apart. Can be sheared at any time, up to three or four times a year. Cut old hedges near the ground to renew.

Lonicera spp.
(honeysuckle)
Informal hedge.
Height 3 to 12 feet.
Sun or partial shade.
Most soils.
Zones 3-9.

Features: Honeysuckles are known for their attractive and often fragrant pink, white, red or yellow flowers and for their red or yellow berries, which are relished by birds but not by humans. They require little maintenance, tolerate urban conditions and are rarely bothered by pests.

Varieties: *L. korolkowii* (blue-leaved honeysuckle, Zones 5-9) grows 12 feet tall and is a good choice in cold climates for a tall hedge. Its showy, dark rose flowers are followed by bright red berries. *L. tatarica* (Tatarian honeysuckle, Zones 3-9), which reaches 8 to 10 feet, is the most widely grown honeysuckle; it has many varieties with white, pink or red flowers. *L. xylosteum* 'Clavey's Dwarf' (Clavey's dwarf honeysuckle, Zones 4 -9), which reaches only 3 to 6 feet, has dense, gray-green leaves, small yellow flowers in spring and red berries in midsummer. *L. xylosteum* 'Hedge King' has finer textured leaves, and can be used as a hedge up to 4 feet high.

Planting and care: Plant 3 feet apart (about 1½ to 2 feet apart for 'Clavey's Dwarf'). Since honeysuckles start to grow very early in the spring, they are best planted in fall.

Philadelphus x *virginalis*
(mock orange)
Informal hedge.
Height to 8 feet.
Full sun to light shade.
Well-drained soil.
Zones 5-9.

Features: An upright, arching form, a fast growth rate and resistance to pests and diseases make mock orange a good choice for an informal screen. Showy white flowers, numerous and sweetly scented, bloom briefly in early summer and are prized for wedding bouquets.

Lavandula angustifolia **(English lavender)**

Varieties: 'True Strain' may bloom all summer long. 'Minnesota Snowflake' can stand temperatures to −30 degrees F.

Planting and care: Plant 2 to 4 feet apart. Prune after flowering, removing stems that have borne blossoms. When plants get leggy (devoid of foliage along their lower stems), cut old wood and unwanted shoots to the ground.

Physocarpus opulifolius
(ninebark)
Formal or informal hedge.
Height 3 to 6 feet.
Sun or partial shade.
Most soils.
Zones 2-8.

Features: Ninebark's fine-textured foliage, made dense by shearing, provides a soft but effective barrier. It tolerates wind, heat, cold and compacted soil.

Varieties: 'Intermedius' is very dense, and turns orange in fall. 'Luteus' is a bigger variety with yellow leaves. 'Nanus' is a fine-

textured dwarf form that grows no higher than 3 feet. 'Dart's Gold' is another dwarf variety with golden yellow leaves. Both can be maintained at 2 feet.
Planting and care: Plant 2 or 3 feet apart (1½ to 2 feet for 'Nanus' and 'Dart's Gold'). Prune twice a year, three or four times if you want a formal hedge.

Populus spp.
(poplar)
Formal hedge or screen.
Height to 60 feet or more.
Full sun to light shade.
Moist, well-drained soil.
Zones 2-10.
Features: *P. nigra* 'Italica' (Lombardy poplar) is the most famous of the poplars for its tall, fast-growing spires of 3-to-4-inch leaves, which turn golden and drop in fall, leaving its upward-facing branches etched against the winter sky. Other handsome columnar varieties, with less height and greater spreads, are *P. alba* 'Bolleana' (Bolleana poplar) and *P. simonii* 'Fastigiata' (pyramidal Simon poplar).
Planting and care: Plant no farther than 8 feet apart for a dense screen. Pruning is generally unnecessary. Locate poplars away from water and sewer lines and septic fields, which their roots will invade.

Potentilla fruticosa
(potentilla, bush cinquefoil)
Informal hedge.
Height 2 to 4 feet.
Full sun to partial shade.

Moist, well-drained soil.
Zones 2-10.
Features: A fine-textured, rounded plant with dark to medium green foliage cut into ½-inch leaflets. With its profuse five-petaled yellow flowers that bloom all summer, potentilla is excellent for a flowering border.
Varieties: 'Jackmannii' is best for hedges, growing up to 4 feet high with a 3-foot spread. 'Gold Star' also makes a neat hedge 2½ feet high. 'Gold Drop' grows 2 feet tall. 'Abbotswood' features pure white flowers on a 2-foot plant. Other cultivars have red, pink or orange blossoms.
Planting and care: Plant 1 to 1½ feet apart. Prune once a year to remove spent flowers.

Prunus maritima
(beach plum)
Informal hedge.
Height 6 to 10 feet.
Full sun.
Well-drained soil.
Zones 4-10.
Features: A dense, rounded shrub particularly suited to seaside locations, the beach plum bears clouds of tiny white flowers and ½-to-1-inch purplish-red fruits that are good for making jelly.
Varieties: *Prunus flava* is similar but bears yellow fruit that is delicious in preserves.
Planting and care: Plant 3 feet apart for a hedge, and up to 6 feet apart for a taller screen. Prune it back the first year to encourage branching; it can be maintained at 4 feet.

Rhamnus frangula 'Columnaris'
(new tallhedge, alder buckthorn)
Formal or informal hedge.
Height to 12 feet.
Sun or partial shade.
Most soils.
Zones 2-8.
Features: With an upright form and fast-growing, dense foliage that needs little pruning, alder buckthorn is a good choice for a screen or hedge. It may grow 10 to 12 feet tall but spread only 4 feet wide. Its leaves are 2 inches long, dark green and shiny; they appear in early spring and do not drop until the late fall. Alder buckthorn flowers are inconspicuous; white berries turn pink, then red. Despite its common name, the plant is thornless.
Planting and care: Plant 2 to 2½ feet apart; it may be sheared to narrower dimensions when planted 1 to 1½ feet apart. When a hedge becomes devoid of foliage along its lower stems, cut it to the ground to renovate it.

Rhus aromatica
(fragrant sumac)
Informal hedge.
Height 3 to 6 feet.
Sun or partial shade.
Most soils.
Zones 3-9.
Features: A tough, adaptable hedge plant, fragrant sumac is good for exposed, windy, dry conditions and restricted sites such as those between a wall and a driveway. Small clusters of red berries are borne in late summer, and the glossy leaves, which

Populus nigra 'Italica' (Lombardy poplars)

smell of spice when crushed, turn red in fall.

Varieties: 'Green Globe' is upright, rounded and better disciplined than the species.

Planting and care: Plant fragrant sumac 4 to 5 feet apart. To restrain its rather floppy growth, shear it twice a year.

Ribes alpinum
(Alpine currant)
Formal or informal hedge.
Height 2 to 5 feet.
Sun or shade.
Most soils.
Zones 3-8.

Features: A graceful low hedge with a dense texture, Alpine currant is a good choice for shady conditions—a tough, low-maintenance, salt-tolerant plant.

Varieties: 'Green Mound', the densest and best cultivar, grows to about 3 feet tall and equally wide. 'Pumilum' makes a good low edging about 2 feet high.

Planting and care: Plant 2 feet apart. Leave unsheared for an informal look, or shear up to three times a year for a more formal hedge.

Rosa hybrids
(rose)
Informal hedge.
Height to 6 feet.
Full sun.
Well-drained, loamy soil.
Zones 3-9.

Features: Beautiful blossoms, which begin in June and continue into fall, provide a continuous supply of cut flowers. The striking red rose hips hang on into

Rosa 'Simplicity'

winter, and can be made into a jelly rich in vitamin C. Thorns make a good barrier against wandering children and dogs.
Varieties: 'Scarlet Mediland', 'Sevillana' and 'Bonica' are some of the newer hybrids that have an extended flowering period and are relatively free of pests and diseases.
Planting and care: Plant 2 feet apart. Fertilize in spring and midsummer. Remove dead, diseased or crossing canes in early spring. Old hedges can be cut back to promote new growth.

Rosa rugosa
(Japanese or saltspray rose)
Informal hedge.
Height 6 to 7 feet.
Full sun.
Well-drained soil.
Zones 3-9.
Features: The lovely magenta blooms cover a hedge in early summer, and flower sporadically into fall. Orange-red hips last all winter. Densely spiny stems make a good barrier. Tolerant of salt spray, wind, cold and polluted air, this plant will grow in sand at the seashore and is pest and disease-free.
Varieties: 'Sir Thomas Lipton' is a double-flowered, fragrant white cultivar that grows up to 5 feet tall. 'Hansa' has sweetly fragrant, double, deep crimson-purple flowers appearing throughout the season. 'F. J. Grootendorst' bears profuse clusters of small double red blooms.
Planting and care: Plant 3 to 4 feet apart. Prune once a year to

eliminate overly thick or damaged stems.

Spiraea spp.
(spiraea)
Informal hedge.
Height to 9 feet.
Sun or partial shade.
Most soils.
Zones 4-10.
Features: Fast growth and abundant flowers in showy, flat-topped clusters make spiraeas good choices for hedges and borders.
Varieties: *S.* x *bumalda* (Bumalda spiraea) comes in several varieties. 'Anthony Waterer' has deep pink flowers and grows 2 feet high. 'Goldflame' has pinkish-red blossoms and grows 2 to 3 feet high. 'Froebelii' has deep pink blossoms and grows 3 to 4 feet high. Among the varieties of *S. japonica* (Japanese spiraea), 'Alpina' bears pink flowers on plants only 1 foot high, 'Coccinea' bears deep crimson blossoms on plants 3 feet high, and 'Atrosanguinea' bears crimson blooms on plants 4 feet tall. *S. nipponica* 'Snowmound' (snowmound or boxwood spiraea) grows in a dense, compact form ideal for hedges 2 to 4 feet high. *S. prunifolia* (bridal-wreath spiraea) has broadly arching branches 5 to 8 feet tall, white buttonlike double flowers and shiny dark green foliage that turns brilliant orange-red in fall. *S.* x *vanhouttei* (Vanhoutte spiraea), the most widely grown spiraea, assumes a fountainlike form 6 to 9 feet high. It is cov-

Spiraea x *bumalda* '**Anthony Waterer**'

ered in late spring by clusters of white flowers that obscure the leaves.
Planting and care: Plant Bumalda and snowmound spiraeas 1½ to 2 feet apart, 'Alpina' 1 foot apart, bridal-wreath and Vanhoutte spiraeas 3 to 8 feet apart. Snowmound, bridalwreath and Vanhoutte spiraeas should be pruned immediately after flowering so that they can produce flowers on the previous season's growth. Prune Bumalda and Japanese spiraeas in early spring before new growth starts so that the current season's stems will produce flowers.

Viburnum dentatum
(arrowwood viburnum)
Informal hedge.
Height 4 to 6 feet.
Sun or partial shade.
Most soils.
Zones 2-9.
Features: This species has flat-topped white flowers in spring,

Spiraea prunifolia (bridalwreath spiraea)

followed by blue fruits and orange-red foliage in fall. Indians used the straight young stems for arrows. This tough plant is good for difficult situations, such as along a driveway or where there are aggressive tree roots.
Planting and care: Plant 2 to 3 feet apart. Remove suckers, fast-growing shoots that grow upright from the shrub's roots.

Viburnum lantana
(wayfaringtree viburnum)
Informal hedge.

Height 5 to 15 feet.
Full sun.
Most soils.
Zones 3-9.
Features: A large hedge plant with all-year interest, way-faringtree viburnum produces lovely white flowers in spring, and fruit clusters that change in color from green to yellow, then to red, blue and finally black in late summer. In late fall, the gray-green leaves turn a rich purplish red.
Varieties: Three good cultivars

are 'Mohican', 'Rugosum' and 'Lee's'.
Planting and care: Plant 4 to 5 feet apart. If you prune at all, do so in winter when you can distinguish between flower and leaf buds (flower buds are generally fatter).

Viburnum trilobum
'Compactum'
(compact American cranberry-bush)
Informal hedge.
Height 3 to 5 feet.

40

Viburnum dentatum (arrowwood viburnum). Overleaf: *Malus* spp. (crabapple) and *Buxus* spp. (boxwood).

Full sun.
Most soils.
Zones 3-9.
Features: The plant makes a low hedge with dense, upright twigs and small, maple-like leaves that turn red in autumn. American cranberrybush's lacy white spring flowers give way to bright red berries that hold on to the branches through the winter and make delicious jams.
Planting and care: Plant 2 to 3 feet apart. Prune to even things up every year or so

Weigela florida
(old-fashioned weigela)
Informal hedge.
Height to 10 feet.
Sun or partial shade.
Most soils.
Zones 5-9.
Features: Arching branches, some of which touch the ground, make weigelas graceful plants. They grow rapidly and bear wide-mouthed flowers an inch or more across in late spring.
Varieties: The species bears pink flowers and grows 9 to 10 feet

tall if left unpruned. Modern hybrids, which rarely exceed 5 to 6 feet, include 'Candida' and 'Bristol Snowflake', white flowers; 'Styriaca', purplish pink; 'Eva Rathke', 'Bristol Ruby' and 'Vanicek', red.
Planting and care: Plant 3 to 8 feet apart, depending on the variety. Since flowers bloom on the previous season's growth, prune immediately after flowering, cutting back to unflowered side branches. Or cut the entire plants back halfway every other year.

EVERGREEN

Abelia x *grandiflora*
(glossy abelia)
Informal or formal hedge.
Height 3 to 10 feet.
Sun or partial shade.
Most soils.
Zones 5-9.
Features: A rounded hedge with small, shiny leaves on many upward-arching stems, glossy abelia has profuse pink or white flowers in late summer to early fall. Usually evergreen, its foliage is reddish bronze in the spring, deep green in the summer and bronze in the fall. Glossy abelia will lose its leaves in winter at the northern end of its range (where it should be grown in a protected spot).
Varieties: 'Sherwoodii' is denser than the species; it grows only about 3 feet tall and equally wide. 'Edward Goucher' grows 3 to 5 feet.
Planting and care: Plant 2 to 4 feet apart. Clip once a year for an informal hedge, up to three times a year for a more formal look (which will reduce the flower display).

Bambusa spp.
(bamboo)
Informal hedge.
Height to 35 feet.
Sun or partial shade.
Most soils.
Zones 8-10.
Features: Bamboos make fine, tall screens and windbreaks because of their fast growth and

ability to thrive in narrow spaces. The leaves produce a pleasing, rustling sound in a breeze.
Varieties: *Bambusa multiplex* (also known as *Bambusa glaucescens*, hedge bamboo) is a clumping variety, staying within bounds (as opposed to a running variety, which spreads invasively to become a pest). *B. multiplex* 'Alphonse Karr' has yellow-green leaves on green-striped yellow canes and grows 10 to 15 feet tall when pruned, 35 feet tall when left alone. *B. multiplex riviereorum* (Chinese goddess bamboo) grows only 8 to 10 feet tall. Another fine ornamental variety is *B. oldhamii* (Oldham bamboo, timber bamboo) with canes up to 3 inches in diameter that may reach 25 feet or more in height.
Planting and care: Plant 2 to 3 feet apart. Water often and deeply, and fertilize monthly for fastest growth. To groom an expanding clump, cut out unwanted canes. To limit height, nip off shoots as they emerge.

Berberis spp.
(barberries)
Informal hedge.
Height 3 to 6 feet.
Sun or partial shade.
Most soils.
Zones 5-9.
Features: Glossy, leathery leaves and abundant thorns make barberries good barriers for children and dogs. Bright yellow flowers in the spring give way to fruits

favored by birds but not by humans.
Varieties: Evergreen barberries will keep their leaves during the winter, providing interest in an otherwise bare landscape. *B.* x *chenaultii* (Chenault barberry) makes a fine low hedge 2 to 4 feet tall. Leaves turn wine-red in fall and hang on through the winter. *B. verruculosa* (warty barberry) makes a handsome barrier up to 4 feet tall; the deep green leaves are white on their undersides. *B. julianae* (wintergreen barberry) grows vigorously up to 5 feet high.
Planting and care: Plant Chenault barberry 2 to 3 feet apart, the others 3 feet apart. Toward the northern end of their range, plant in a protected spot away from drying winter winds. Shear once a year.

Buxus spp.
(boxwood)
Formal hedge.
Height 3 to 8 feet.
Sun or shade.
Cool, moist soil.
Zones 4-10.
Features: Fine-textured, slow-growing and long-lived, boxwood hedges have been grown by Americans for more than two hundred years, and have been shaped into topiary figures ranging from dogs to ducks. *B. sempervirens* (common boxwood, English box) and *B. microphylla* var. *japonica* can be maintained as

Ilex opaca 'Brilliantissima' (American Holly) *with Juniperus chinensis* 'Pfitzerana Gold Star' (yellow-green foliage) *and Juniperus horizontalis* 'Wiltonii' (blue rug juniper, blue-green foliage)

sheared hedges 4 to 8 feet tall. *B. microphylla* var. *koreana* (Korean littleleaf box) can be maintained at 1 to 1½ feet high.

Varieties: Two of the best hybrids are 'Green Mountain' and 'Green Velvet', which grow to about 3½ feet tall. 'Winter Gem' holds its dark green color well in northern climates, as does 'Green Beauty', which grows 4 to 6 feet high.

Planting and care: Plant 1 to 2 feet apart in soil with a high proportion of organic matter, to provide moisture retention and good drainage. Mulch the plants to keep the roots cool and moist. In the north, try to plant in a protected spot out of drying winter winds. Fertilize in spring to speed up the plants' rather slow growth.

Cupressocyparis leylandii **(cupressocyparis)**
Formal or informal hedge.
Height to 30 feet or more.
Sun.
Most soils.

Zones 6-9.

Features: A fast-growing needled evergreen tree with a narrow, upright, pyramidal form, cupressocyparis can be sheared to maintain it at 4-5 feet.

Varieties: The foliage of 'Castelwellian Gold' has a yellowish cast.

Planting and care: Plant 2 to 4 feet apart for a sheared hedge, to 6 feet apart for a tall screen. Shear at any time.

Euonymus japonicus
(evergreen euonymus)
Formal or informal hedge.
Height 6 to 10 feet.
Sun or partial shade.
Most soils.
Zones 6-10.

Features: A densely branching, upright shrub with dark green, glossy leaves 1 to 2½ inches long. Inconspicuous flowers are followed by small but showy pink-to-orange inedible berries in fall.

Varieties: 'Grandifolia' has larger, darker green leaves. 'Albo-marginatus' has white-edged leaves. 'Aureo-marginatus' has yellow-edged leaves. The leaves of 'Aureo-variegatus' are green at the edges and yellow at the center. 'Microphyllus' is a compact variety, no taller than 2 feet, that seldom needs pruning.

Planting and care: Plant 1 to 2 feet apart for a sheared hedge, to 3 feet apart for an informal screen. Prune at any time.

Gardenia jasminoides
(gardenia)
Informal hedge.

Height 4 to 8 feet.
Full sun (partial shade in hot areas).
Slightly acid, well-drained soil.
Zones 8-10.

Features: Gardenias are valued for their shiny dark green leaves and large, sweetly fragrant 3-inch flowers.

Varieties: Among the best are 'Veitchii', which bears many flowers on upright branches 4 to 5 feet tall; 'August Beauty', which grows 4 to 6 feet tall; and 'Mystery', which has large flowers on plants 6 to 8 feet high.

Planting and care: Plant 1 to 2 feet apart, placing plants at the same depth as they were growing in the container to an inch higher. Mulch with 2 or 3 inches of wood chips or ground bark. For impressive results, feed with acid plant food once a month.

Ilex spp.
(holly)
Informal or formal hedges.
Height 1 to 20 feet or more.
Sun or partial shade.
Slightly acid, well-drained soil.
Zones 5-10.

Features: Evergreen hollies, which come in hundreds of varieties, make outstanding hedge and screening plants. Their flowers are inconspicuous, but many varieties bear ornamental red, yellow or white berries, which in some species are poisonous.

Varieties: *I.* x *altaclarensis* 'Wilsonii' (Wilson's holly, Zones 6-10), which grows 6 to 8 feet high, has shiny, spiny-edged leaves 3 to 5 inches long and

bears bright red berries in profusion. *I. aquifolium* (English holly, Zones 6-9), which grows 6 to 30 feet tall, has red berries and spiny leaves 1½ to 3 inches long. *I. cornuta* (Chinese holly, Zones 6-10), which grows 4 to 10 feet tall, comes in an excellent variety, 'Burfordii', which has spineless 4-inch leaves and large orange-red berries; 'D'Or' produces heavy crops of yellow berries. *I. crenata* (Japanese holly, Zones 5-10) grows 1 to 8 feet high; its ½- to 1-inch leaves accept shearing well. Among others are *I. opaca* (American holly, Zones 5-9), which comes in many varieties, and *I. vomitoria* (yaupon, Zones 7-10), which has 1-inch leaves that tolerate shearing; a dwarf variety, 'Nana', can be maintained at 1½ to 3 feet tall.

Planting and care: Plant 1 to 4 feet apart, depending on variety. Choose a self-fertile cultivar, or use at least one male plant for every 10 females. A wind-protected site in colder areas will avoid frost damage. Mulch with a 2-inch layer of wood chips or ground bark. Prune to shape in late spring after growth is complete.

Ilex glabra 'Compacta'
(compact inkberry holly)
Informal or formal hedge.
Height 3 to 6 feet.
Sun or partial shade.
Acid soil.
Zones 3-9.

Features: The hardiest broad-leaved evergreen available to northern gardeners. A fine-

Kalmia latifolia (mountain laurel)

textured hedge consisting of many small, shiny, dark green leaves that turn brownish green in winter, inkberry holly bears abundant black, pea-sized inedible berries. Resistant to pests and diseases, it is a good choice for the seashore.

Varieties: *Ilex glabra* 'Densa', a winner of the 1994 Pennsylvania Horticultural Society's Gold Medal Plant Award, stays denser and fuller than others of the species, growing about 6 feet tall.

Planting and care: Plant 3 feet apart. Fertilize in spring beginning the year after planting. Shear once in summer to achieve a formal look. Cut back suckers, fast-growing shoots that grow upright from the shrub's roots.

Juniperus chinensis
(Chinese juniper)
Semiformal or formal hedge.
Height to 20 feet.
Full sun.
Most soils.

Zones 4-9.

Features: The evergreen foliage of this plant, available in several dozen cultivars, is needled or scale-like, and can be any shade of green as well as blue, silver or gray.

Varieties: 'Columnaris' forms a narrow cone with dense blue-green foliage. 'Hetzi' is a fast-growing variety with bluish foliage. 'Keteleeri' grows into a broad conical tree with bright green foliage. Other good choices are 'Ames', 'Blue Point', 'Mountbatten', 'Iowa', and 'Fairview'.

Planting and care: Plant 2 to 4 feet apart. Prune at any time, making the hedge wider at the base. Chinese junipers have a tendency to lose their lower foliage unless they are carefully pruned.

Juniperus virginiana
(Eastern red cedar)
Semiformal or formal hedge.
Height 5 to 25 feet.
Full sun.
Most soils.
Zones 2-10.

Features: The native equivalent of the Chinese juniper, the red cedar is hardier. It also has foliage varying from light to dark green, blue, silver or gray. Red cedar makes a good windbreak and grows under urban conditions.

Varieties: *J. virginiana* 'Canaertii', Canaert red cedar, holds its rich dark green color through the winter. 'Hillspire', a narrow variety, has dense bright

green foliage all year. 'Manhattan Blue', with blue-green needles, is very compact. *J. virginiana pyramidalis hillii*, called Dundee juniper, is narrowly conical and slow-growing. Its foliage is grayish green in summer, purple in winter.

Planting and care: Plant 2 to 3 feet apart. The species' compact habit can be accentuated by a light shearing with hedge shears at any time.

Kalmia latifolia
(mountain laurel)
Informal hedge.
Height 3 to 7 feet.
Full sun to deep shade.
Well drained, acid soil.
Zones 4-8.

Features: Though not often thought of as a hedge plant, mountain laurel can be massed with spectacular effects. The evergreen leaves, which are poisonous, are always graceful, and the display of pink, white or red flowers is stunning in June.

Planting and care: Plant 2 to 3 feet apart. Mulch with a 2-to-3-inch layer of wood chips, leaves or ground bark. Spindly plants can be cut back to just above the ground and will send out new shoots.

Laurus nobilis
(sweet bay, Grecian laurel)
Formal or informal hedge.
Height to 20 feet or more.
Full sun or part shade.
Most well-drained soils.
Zones 8-10.

Features: A classic hedge plant

Kalmia latifolia 'Nipmonk' (mountain laurel)

Nerium oleander (oleander)

of the Renaissance gardens of Italy, sweet bay has multiple stems and a broad, conical form. Its dense, dark green leaves (2 to 4 inches wide and 1 inch long) are pungent when crushed—the "bay leaf" used in cooking. It tolerates city conditions.

Planting and care: Plant 1 to 3 feet apart for a sheared hedge, which can be maintained at 4 feet. Plant up to 6 feet apart for a taller screen. Shear when new growth becomes 3 to 4 inches long.

Ligustrum spp.

(privet)
Formal or informal hedge.
Height 6 to 15 feet.
Sun or partial shade.
Most soils.
Zones 7-10.

Features: Evergreen privets are fast-growing, pest-free shrubs that are widely used for hedges, screens and shrub borders.

Varieties: *L. japonicum* (Japanese privet) is one of the most popular hedge plants in mild climates. It has shiny, thick, spongy leaves 2 to 4 inches long and showy, pungent-smelling white flowers in summer, followed by small blue-black berries. *L. lucidum* (glossy privet, Zones 8-10) has 3-to-6-inch leaves and flower clusters up to 9 inches across, followed by masses of berries.

Planting and care: Plant 1 to 3 feet apart. Shear formal hedges just as growth starts, and again when shoots are 3 to 4 inches long. Sheared plants will bear fewer flowers.

Lonicera nitida

(box honeysuckle)
Formal hedge.
Height to 6 feet.
Sun to partial shade.
Most soils.
Zones 7-10.

Features: This plant looks more like a boxwood than a honeysuckle when neatly sheared. Its ½-inch leaves are shiny, dark green and oval-shaped. Box honeysuckle bears small, fragrant white flowers and purplish, translucent inedible berries; its leaves turn bronze in cold weather.

Planting and care: Plant 1 to 3 feet apart for a sheared hedge. Shear as often as needed for a neat appearance.

Nandina domestica

(nandina, heavenly bamboo)
Informal hedge.
Height to 6 feet.
Sun to shade.
Most soils.
Zones 6-10.

Features: Nandina is a delicate-looking, upright plant resembling bamboo, with many 1-to-2-inch pointed leaflets. Its small white flowers appear in clusters, followed by red berries relished by birds. Leaf color in winter is often bright red.

Varieties: 'Compacta' grows 4 to 5 feet high. 'Nana' forms mounds up to 18 inches high and is redder than the species; it is useful in borders. 'Alba' has white berries.

Planting and care: Plant 1½ to 2½ feet apart, 'Nana' 12 to 18 inches apart. Add a mulch over

Lonicera nitida 'Baggessen's Gold' (box honeysuckle)

roots in areas with hot summers. Do not shear, but thin out canes instead. The plant is deciduous where winters drop to 10 degrees F, but no lower.

Nerium oleander

(oleander)
Informal hedge or screen.
Height to 12 feet or more.
Full sun.
Most soils.
Zones 8-10.

Features: Grown in ancient Persia and Moorish Spain, oleanders make a classic warm-climate screen with their lance-like leaves and 2-inch fragrant, showy flowers, colored white, pink, salmon or red. All parts of the plant are poisonous if eaten.

Varieties: Among many cultivars are 'Sealy Pink', 'Red Single' and 'Cherry Ripe' (rose red). Smaller-growing varieties, to 6 feet, include 'Mrs. Roeding' (double salmon), 'Casablanca' (white) and 'Algiers' (dark red). Dwarfs, which can be held to 3 to 5 feet high or less, are 'Petite Pink' and 'Petite Salmon'.

Planting and care: Plant 2 to 3 feet apart, to 6 feet apart for a screen. Prune in early spring.

Osmanthus heterophyllus
(false holly)
Informal or formal hedge.
Height to 20 feet.
Tolerates shade.
Most soils.
Zones 6-10.
Features: The plant has hollylike foliage, with 2-inch dark green, spiny leaves. Like hollies, its fragrant yellow flowers are inconspicuous.
Varieties: 'Gulftide' grows 15 feet high, 'Ilicifolius' 20 feet high. 'Variegatus' grows slowly to 5 feet and has leaves edged in white; 'Aureus' is similar but smaller. *Osmanthus fragrans* (sweet olive), a related species that grows in Zones 8-10, has leaves 4 inches long and blooms fragrantly all year in areas with mild winters.
Planting and care: Plant 1½ to 3 feet apart for a sheared hedge, 3 to 4 feet apart for a more informal hedge. Can be maintained at 5 feet. Do major shaping in early spring, but the plant can be sheared at any time.

Photinia x fraseri
(photinia)
Informal or formal hedge.
Height to 12 feet.
Sun or partial shade.
Most soils.

Zones 7-10.
Features: Photinia is most notable for its glossy 3-to-5-inch leaves, which when new are bright red. Shearing enhances the effect. Clusters of small white flowers are profuse and showy in spring.
Planting and care: Plant 3 to 4 feet apart. Shape at any time. Tolerates heat and drought.

Picea spp.
(spruce)
Screen or windbreak.
Height to 30 feet or more.
Full sun.
Rich, moist soil.
Zones 2-10.
Features: Fast-growing and cold-tolerant, spruces are valued as windbreaks and privacy screens where there is space enough for them. *P. abies* (Norway spruce) is a large, cone-shaped tree with dark green needles. *P. glauca* (white spruce) is also large and cone-shaped but has pale or grayish-green needles.
Varieties: Compact forms of white spruce include 'Conica' (dwarf Alberta spruce), which is very slow-growing to 8 feet tall, and 'Densata' (Black Hills spruce), which grows slowly to 20 feet or more.
Planting and care: Plant 3 feet apart for a sheared hedge, 10 feet or more for a tall screen. Prune in early spring. Spruces can be maintained at 6 feet.

Pinus strobus
(Eastern white pine)
Screen or windbreak.

Pinus strobus **(Eastern white pine)**

Height to 20 feet or more.
Full sun.
Most soils.
Zones 3-8.
Features: A soft-textured, fast-growing tree, the white pine makes an effective screen at property lines. Once established, it requires little care. It does best in a well-drained, acid soil that is moist and fertile.
Varieties: *P. strobus* 'Fastigiata' is a narrower, columnar cultivar.
Planting and care: Plant 3 to 6 feet apart. To keep a hedge low, prune annually. Higher hedges should be pruned every second year. When new shoots of growth, called "candles" appear in spring, cut each to half its length.

Podocarpus macrophyllus
(yew podocarpus, yew pine)
Formal hedge or screen.
Height to 20 feet.
Full sun or light shade (the latter is preferable where summers are hot).

Pyracantha coccinea (firethorn)

Taxus cuspidata (**Japanese yew**)

Moist, well drained soil. Zones 7-10.

Features: Similar to yews, yew podocarpuses make an unusually upright, tall, narrow, sheared hedge, ideal where space is limited. Their needles are 3 to 4 inches long.

Varieties: *P. macrophyllus* var. *maki* (shrubby or Chinese podocarpus) is smaller and slower-growing, reaching a height of 6 to 8 feet. It can also be maintained at 3 to 4 feet, and is a popular indoor plant.

Planting and care: Plant 1 to 3 feet apart for a sheared hedge, 3 to 4 feet apart for a taller screen. Shear two or three times a year during the growing season.

Prunus caroliniana (Carolina cherry laurel)

Informal or formal hedge or screen.
Height to 20 feet or more.
Full sun to partial shade.
Well-drained soil.
Zones 7-10.

Features: A dense, fast-growing plant with dark green leaves up to 3 inches long, Carolina cherry's fruits are small green cherries that turn black as they mature in summer. Berries, leaves and bark are poisonous.

Varieties: 'Compacta' and 'Bright 'n Tight' are smaller than the species, grow more slowly and are better behaved.

Planting and care: Plant 2 feet apart for a sheared hedge, 6 feet apart for a taller screen. Can be maintained at 3 feet. Prune whenever necessary to keep neat and to eliminate messy flowers and fruit.

Prunus laurocerasus
(cherry laurel, English laurel)
Informal hedge or screen.
Height to 20 feet or more.
Full sun to partial shade.
Most soils.
Zones 5-9.
Features: English laurel is a coarse-textured, fast-growing, long-lived plant. Its dark green oval leaves may reach up to 7 inches long, and its fruits are small green cherries that turn purple as they mature. It tolerates city conditions. Cherries, leaves and bark are poisonous if eaten.
Varieties: 'Schipkaensis' can stand cold to Zone 5. 'Otto Luykens' is a compact, more refined form with smaller leaves; 'Zabeliana' is broad and spreading with narrow leaves. Both of the latter grow to about 6 feet.
Planting and care: Plant 3 feet apart for a hedge, up to 8 feet apart for a taller screen. Cherry laurels can be sheared with hedge shears or can be shaped by pruning individual branches by hand.

Pseudotsuga menziesii
(Douglas fir)
Screen or windbreak.
Height to 20 feet or more.
Full sun.
Moist, well-drained soil.
Zones 4-9.
Features: Most familiar as free-standing, conical Christmas trees, Douglas firs tolerate shearing and can be planted close together to form a tall screen or hedge. Fast-growing when young, they shoot up 1 to 2 feet a year. Their soft, aromatic blue-green needles and their branches form a good barrier.
Planting and care: Plant 2 feet apart for a sheared hedge, up to 8 feet apart for a taller screen. Shape with hedge shears in early spring before new growth begins.

Pyracantha coccinea
(scarlet firethorn)
Informal hedge.
Height 6 to 14 feet.
Full sun.
Most soils.
Zones 6-10.
Features: Noted for its spectacular display of white flowers in late spring and its masses of orange-red berries in fall and winter, firethorn's evergreen leaves turn brown or drop near the northern edge of its range in winter. It requires frequent pruning to be neat (avoid the small but painful thorns), but is a fine barrier hedge.
Varieties: *P. coccinea* 'Lalandei', Laland firethorn, is one of the most popular berried shrubs in America. Similar varieties include 'Mohave', 'Fiery Candles' and 'Government Red'. 'Lowboy' is a spreading variety, growing only 3 feet tall but 6 feet across.
Planting and care: Plant 2 to 3 feet apart. Its fast growth rate requires constant shaping.

Santolina chamaecyparissus
(lavender cotton)
Low border or hedge.
Height to 2 feet.

Pseudotsuga menziesii
(Douglas fir)

Full sun.
Well-drained soil.
Zones 7-10.
Features: Silvery, woolly foliage and tiny, bright yellow flowers in summer make this plant a good choice for edging a path or a flower bed. The flowers and aromatic foliage, which yield a perfume oil, can be used in dried arrangements or hung in the closet as a moth repellent.
Planting and care: Plant 1 to 1½ feet apart for a border, to 2 feet apart for a low, shaped hedge.

Taxus cuspidata
(Japanese yew);
Taxus x media
(intermediate yew)
Formal or informal hedge or border.
Height to 20 feet.
Sun or shade.
Most well-drained soils.
Zones 4-8.
Features: A popular, durable hedge plant, with flat, soft, waxy

Tsuga canadensis
(Canada hemlock)

needles and bright red berries. Plants can be pruned informally or sheared for a formal appearance. Berries, leaves and bark are poisonous.

Varieties: For low borders, 1 to 3 feet tall, choose *Taxus cuspidata* 'Nana' or 'Minima', or *Taxus* x *media* 'Chadwick', 'Brownii' or 'Wardii'. For medium tall hedges, there are *Taxus cuspidata* 'Jeffrey's Pyramidal' and *Taxus* x *media* 'Hatfieldii', 'Amherstii', 'Stovekenii', 'Kelseyi' or 'Hicksii'. For tall, narrow hedges, try *Taxus cuspidata* 'Capitata' or *Taxus* x *media* 'Sentinalis'.

Planting and care: Plant 2 to 5 feet apart, depending on size. For an informal effect, prune once a year, using hand clippers to remove long branches from within the plants. For a formal hedge, shear with hedge shears early in the growing season, and once or twice more if necessary to keep the hedge neat.

Teucrium chamaedrys
(germander)
Formal or informal border.
Height 1 to 8 feet.
Sun or partial shade.
Well-drained soil.
Zones 6-10.
Features: Once used in medieval knot gardens and as a medicinal herb, germander is useful for low edgings where it is too sunny and warm for boxwood. The leaves, ¾ inch long or less, are easily sheared. Spikes of its purplish or white flowers are attractive to bees.
Varieties: *T. fruticans* (bush germander) grows 4 to 8 feet high and can be used for larger shaped hedges.
Planting and care: Plant 1 to 1½ feet apart. Shear at least once a year in early spring to keep it neat.

Thuja occidentalis
(American aborvitae)
Formal hedge.
Height to 20 feet.
Sun to partial shade.
Moist soil.
Zones 2-8.
Features: Arborvitae is a fine, low-maintenance hedge, neat of habit and slow of growth. Its popularity accounts for the great variety of cultivars available.
Varieties: 'Globosa' or 'Woodwardii' make pretty, undulating hedges about 4 feet tall. 'Hetz Midget' is a lower variety, good for edging. 'Little Gem' makes a rounded hedge up to 8 feet high. 'Emerald', 'Techny' and 'Nigra' are upright arborvitaes best kept at 5 to 10 feet.
Planting and care: Plant 18 inches

to 3 feet apart, depending on the variety. Keep them mulched, and feed young plants to speed growth. Arborvitaes can be sheared, but rarely need it. Selective pruning can be done at any time.

Tsuga canadensis
(Canada hemlock)
Informal to semiformal hedge, windbreak or screen.
Height to 20 feet or more.
Sun or partial shade.
Well-drained, moist, acid soil.
Zones 3-7.
Features: There is nothing quite so graceful as a hemlock hedge, with its sprays of tiny, flat needles. It is a lovely choice, and durable, too.
Planting and care: Plant 4 feet apart. For a soft effect, prune every other year. For a more formal look, prune annually after new growth in June. To ensure the growth of lower foliage, remember to shape plants wider at the base.

Thuja occidentalis (arborvitae) and
Juniperus virginiana (red cedar)

Pinus strobus (Eastern white pine)

A LIST OF SPECIES BY FUNCTION

Formal Hedges

Abelia x *grandiflora*
(glossy abelia)

Acanthopanax sieboldianus
(five-leaf aralia)

Acer campestre (hedge maple)

Berberis spp. (barberry)

Buxus spp. (boxwood)

Cornus mas (cornelian cherry)

Cotoneaster lucidus
(hedge cotoneaster)

Cupressocyparis leylandii
(cupressocyparis)

Euonymus alata
(winged euonymus,
burning bush)

Euonymus japonicus
(evergreen euonymus)

Fagus sylvatica
(European beech)

Ilex spp. (holly)

Ilex glabra 'Compacta'
(compact inkberry holly)

Juniperus chinensis
(Chinese juniper)

Laurus nobilis (sweet bay,
Grecian laurel)

Ligustrum spp. (privet)

Ligustrum amurense
(Amur privet)

Lonicera nitida
(box honeysuckle)

Osmanthus heterophyllus
(false holly)

Photinia x *fraseri* (photinia)

Physocarpus opulifolius
(ninebark)

Podocarpus macrophyllus (yew
podocarpus, yew pine)

Populus spp. (poplar)

Prunus caroliniana
(Carolina cherry laurel)

Rhamnus frangula
'Columnaris' (new tallhedge,
alder buckthorn)

Ribes alpinum (Alpine currant)

Taxus cuspidata (Japanese yew)

Taxus x *media*
(intermediate yew)

Teucrium chamaedrys
(germander)

Thuja occidentalis
(American aborvitae)

Tsuga canadensis
(Canada hemlock)

Informal Hedges

Abelia x *grandiflora*
(glossy abelia)

Acanthopanax sieboldianus
(five-leaf aralia)

Acer campestre (hedge maple)

Acer ginnala (Amur maple)

Artemisia abrotanum
(southernwood)

Bambusa spp. (bamboo)

Berberis spp. (barberry)

Chaenomeles speciosa
(flowering quince)

Clethra alnifolia (summersweet, sweet pepper bush)

Cornus mas (cornelian cherry)

Cornus racemosa
(gray dogwood)

Cornus sericea (red osier
dogwood)

Cotoneaster lucidus
(hedge cotoneaster)

Crataegus crus-galli

(cockspur hawthorn)

Cupressocyparis leylandii
(cupressocyparis)

Elaeagnus angustifolia
(Russian olive)

Euonymus alata (winged
euonymus, burning bush)

Euonymus japonicus
(evergreen euonymus)

Fagus sylvatica
(European beech)

Forsythia x *intermedia*
(border forsythia)

Gardenia jasminoides
(gardenia)

Hibiscus syriacus (rose of
Sharon, shrub althea)

Ilex spp. (holly)

Ilex glabra 'Compacta'
(compact inkberry holly)

Ilex verticillata (winterberry)

Kalmia latifolia
(mountain laurel)

Laurus nobilis (sweet bay,
Grecian laurel)

Ligustrum spp. (privet)

Ligustrum amurense
(Amur privet)

Lonicera spp. (honeysuckle)

Nandina domestica (nandina,
heavenly bamboo)

Nerium oleander (oleander)

Osmanthus heterophyllus
(false holly)

Philadelphus x *virginalis*
(mock orange)

Photinia x *fraseri* (photinia)

Physocarpus opulifolius
(ninebark)

Potentilla fruticosa (potentilla,

bush cinquefoil)

Prunus caroliniana
   (Carolina cherry laurel)

Prunus laurocerasus (cherry
   laurel, English laurel)

Prunus maritima (beach plum)

Pyracantha coccinea (firethorn)

Rhamnus frangula
   'Columnaris' (new tallhedge,
   alder buckthorn)

Rhus aromatica
   (fragrant sumac)

Ribes alpinum (Alpine currant)

Rosa hybrids (rose)

Rosa rugosa (Japanese or
   saltspray rose)

Spiraea spp. (spiraea)

Taxus cuspidata (Japanese yew)

Taxus x *media*
   (intermediate yew)

Tsuga canadensis
   (Canada hemlock)

Viburnum dentatum
   (arrowwood viburnum)

Viburnum lantana (wayfaringtree viburnum)

Viburnum trilobum
   'Compactum' (compact
   American cranberrybush)

Weigela florida (old-fashioned
   weigela)

Low Borders

Artemisia abrotanum
   (southernwood)

Buxus spp. (boxwood)

Ilex spp. (holly)

Lavandula (lavender)

Nandina domestica (nandina,
   heavenly bamboo)

Potentilla fruticosa (potentilla,
   bush cinquefoil)

Ribes alpinum (Alpine currant)

Santolina chamaecyparissus
   (lavender cotton)

Taxus cuspidata (Japanese yew)

Taxus x *media*
   (intermediate yew)

Teucrium chamaedrys
   (germander)

High Screens and Windbreaks

Acer campestre (hedge maple)

Bambusa spp. (bamboo)

Crataegus crus-galli
   (cockspur hawthorn)

Cupressocyparis leylandii
   (cupressocyparis)

Fagus sylvatica
   (European beech)

Ilex spp. (holly)

Juniperus chinensis
   (Chinese juniper)

Juniperus virginiana
   (Eastern red cedar)

Laurus nobilis (sweet bay,
   Grecian laurel)

Nerium oleander (oleander)

Osmanthus heterophyllus
   (false holly)

Picea spp. (spruce)

Pinus strobus (Eastern
   white pine)

Podocarpus macrophyllus
   (yew podocarpus, yew pine)

Populus spp. (poplar)

Prunus caroliniana
   (Carolina cherry laurel)

Prunus laurocerasus (cherry
   laurel, English laurel)

Pseudotsuga menziesii
   (Douglas fir)

Tsuga canadensis

(Canada hemlock)

Thorny Barriers

Acanthopanax sieboldianus
   (five-leaf aralia)

Berberis spp. (barberry)

Crataegus crus-galli
   (cockspur hawthorn)

Pyracantha coccinea (firethorn)

Rosa hybrids (rose)

Rosa rugosa (Japanese or
   saltspray rose)

Flowering Hedges

Abelia x *grandiflora*
   (glossy abelia)

Chaenomeles speciosa
   (flowering quince)

Clethra alnifolia (summersweet, sweet pepper bush)

Forsythia x *intermedia*
   (border forsythia)

Gardenia jasminoides
   (gardenia)

Hibiscus syriacus (rose of
   Sharon, shrub althea)

Kalmia latifolia
   (mountain laurel)

Lonicera spp. (honeysuckle)

Nerium oleander (oleander)

Philadelphus x *virginalis*
   (mock orange)

Potentilla fruticosa
   (potentilla, bush cinquefoil)

Pyracantha coccinea (firethorn)

Rosa hybrids (rose)

Rosa rugosa (Japanese or
   saltspray rose)

Spiraea spp. (spiraea)

Weigela florida (old-fashioned
   weigela)

CHAPTER TWO

VINES
VERSATILE CLIMBERS

INES ARE THE MOST VERSATILE living fences.
They can screen an unwanted view as effectively as
a solid wood fence while allowing the passage of light
and air. They may be used to soften the harsh lines
of a blank wall, to conceal an unattractive chain-link
fence or to screen a vegetable garden or work yard from the rest of
the garden. Vines put on a maximum display of flowers and foliage
while taking up very little ground area, a plus for those without the
space or the funds needed to plant a hedge. And unlike hedges, vines
can be a temporary solution for a homeowner with a view to screen,
a quick fix while a more permanent plan is implemented.

Long ago, vines became scandent—from the Latin *scandere*, to
climb—in order to compete for light. They have developed an
ingenious variety of ways to surmount any obstacles to the sunlight
they require. Some species like cape honeysuckles are "leaners,"
reclining against other plants or objects unless tied to trellises to keep
them upright. "Hookers" like rambler roses have thorns that keep
their stems from backsliding by catching onto anything they touch,
though they still have to be tied to supports. Star jasmine and other

"weavers" hold themselves up by growing in and out of a support like wire mesh. "Rooters," among them English ivy and climbing hydrangea, produce clusters of small roots that anchor the vine in any rough spot or crack they can find. "Twiners" like morning glories, wisterias and sweet peas go around and around the nearest vertical support, guided by their sensitive growing tips (some vines, like Chinese wisteria, climb by twining from left to right; others, like Japanese wisteria, twine from right to left). "Clingers" like clematis and grapevines

Roses (Rosa spp.) *are "hookers," vines whose thorns catch onto the climbing surface. Previous page: Trellised climbing roses add a vertical note to the garden.*

climb by means of tendrils—delicate, thread-like organs that coil around anything in their way. "Stickers" like Boston ivy develop small adhesive disks that stick fast to any rough surface.

Another asset to vines in their search for sunlight is their ability to grow quickly. Certain species of clematis may elongate as much as 18 or 20 feet in a season. Grapevines can put on 30 or 40 feet. An extreme example—one you'll want to avoid—is kudzu, which has earned a reputation as "the vine that ate the South." Kudzu produces shoots 60 feet long in a single

growing season. Introduced from Asia in the 1930s as a ground cover to save eroding lands, this member of the pea family has gone berserk, taking over not only the cut banks where it was originally planted but fields, woodlands and buildings as well.

CHOOSING A VINE

IN CHOOSING A VINE for a particular purpose, you should bear in mind how fast it will grow, how large it can get, what kind of support it will need and whether it is deciduous or will remain evergreen year round. You may want to consider the size and shape of leaves, the color and timing of flowers and berries and whether the foliage turns an attractive color in fall. Most important is whether or not it will grow in the area in which you live, whether it needs full sun or can stand partial shade, and whether it has special requirements regarding soil. For specific information, see the descriptions of particular species in this chapter, and the Zone Map on pages 120-121.

In general, vines prefer temperate areas. If you live in chilly Zone 3, which includes the southern part of Canada and the northern parts of Montana, North Dakota, Minnesota and Wisconsin, there are still a handful of perennial vines you can grow, among them American bittersweet, trumpet honeysuckle and Virginia creeper. Zone 4, which includes the Plains states and northern Maine, adds more, such as five-leaf akebia and porcelain berry, but it is in Zone 5 and southward that the selection expands—clematis, Japanese wisteria, porcelain ampelopsis, climbing hydrangea and silver lace vine, to name a few.

Most vines will produce their largest leaves and most prolific flowers in full sun. Spreading the vines over an expanse of sunny wall or training them up a freestanding fence or trellis encourages the formation of flower buds. The exceptions to this rule are vines like English ivy

Clematis (Clematis hybrida), *a sturdy flowering perennial vine, softens the outlines of a solid fence. This woody vine grows in several zones and prefers partial shade.*

and wintercreeper, which can die back due to the drying effects of excess winter sun, and for which a northern or eastern exposure is favored in regions with cold winters. If you have a shady situation, however, do not despair. Several vines will grow in partial shade, including clematis, euonymus, climbing hydrangea, honeysuckle, grape, actinidia, five-leaf akebia, Virginia creeper and Dutchman's pipe.

One common use for vines is to disguise a chain-link fence, whether erected on a property line for security or around a swimming pool to comply with a local zoning code. A large-leaved, fast-growing grapevine or Dutchman's pipe will soon bury such a fence under cascades of foliage. A lighter effect can be had by using five-leaf akebia, trumpet vine or silver lace vine, all of which will provide masses of flowers as an added bonus. A quick camouflage can be achieved with a vigorous annual vine like morning glory, which will cover an unattractive surface until a slower-growing perennial vine becomes established.

VINES ON FREESTANDING TRELLISES can be used to screen one area from another. Alongside an outdoor sitting area, for example, a vine can cut off an unwelcome view of the neighbors, separate a play space cluttered with children's toys, or block off a service yard. If the vine is encouraged to grow overhead on a trellis or pergola as well, it can provide pleasant, sun-dappled shade.

While planting vines next to a house, remember that the soil near the foundation may be alkaline from lime leaching out of the concrete, or may contain rubble used as backfill. You may have to dig out and completely replace this soil with new topsoil enriched with a generous amount of compost or leaf mold. Remember, too, that a vine planted next to a house wall may be denied rain by an overhanging eave and thus will need additional watering. If you have a gutterless roof, do not locate a vine directly under the drip line, where water pouring off the roof can injure the plant.

Various vines can be used to cover an expanse of bare wall, which, if southerly-facing, will expose the vine to maximum light and warmth, producing rich displays of foliage and flowers. If the wall is of stone or brick, Boston or English ivy or Virginia creeper will need no help in climbing it. On smoother surfaces, such as

A long-lived vine that needs the sturdy support this arbor provides, wisteria requires partial shade and plenty of moisture.

English ivy's aerial rootlets grasp onto brick and stone walls easily, and it will quickly cover any wall, given the opportunity. On a smoother surface, such as concrete blocks or poured concrete, it may be necessary to string horizontal wires before planting so the vines can get a better grip.

painted concrete blocks or poured concrete, they may need horizontal wires, installed before the vines are planted, strung every few feet to support their weight. Use copper wire, which weathers to an unobtrusive dark color, or electrical wire covered with dark green or black plastic. Before planting, hammer masonry nails into the joints of the masonry, or use a masonry drill to make holes into which you can set expanding lead anchors and rustproof hooks, eye screws or lag screws every few feet. Then stretch lengths of wire tautly between the supports, incorporating turnbuckles at one or both ends to

take up the slack as the plants mature and grow heavier, straining the wires. Wires are desirable on any surface for heavy, sticking vines like climbing hydrangeas, which project out from the wall and may be torn away in a stiff wind unless anchored to a wire.

DO NOT USE STICKING or clinging vines, such as English or Boston ivy, on a wall of wooden shingles or clapboards. In search of moisture to make their tentacles stick, they pry into crevices and promote rot. And if any repainting is needed, the vines have to be ripped down. You can, however, grow vines against wood—if you take care to separate the two. A light twining vine like the cup-and-saucer vine needs nothing more than a vertical copper wire, or a parallel series of wires, stretched between an overhanging eave and stakes driven into the ground so that the vines will grow 6 inches or more out from the wall. Or you can use a framework of wood with wires or nylon cord lashed to it, or wide-mesh, plastic-coated wire fencing, or even chicken wire, which will soon be concealed by the growing foliage.

For a more permanent and nicer-looking support, garden centers stock different kinds of prefabricated trellises made of aluminum, plastic or wood. Or you can build your own out of light lumber. You can paint it white, or the color of your house; if you use a rot-resistant wood like cedar, redwood or cypress, it can be left unpainted and will weather to a pleasing drift-wood gray.

If your wall is wood, don't secure the trellis directly to it. Leave a few inches of space between the wall and a smaller vine, and 6 inches for a large vine, to allow for the free circulation of air between the vine and the wall. Air circulation prevents rot and discourages fungus growth, and moving the vine away from the wall makes it easier to prune. Use angle irons or short blocks of wood to secure the trellis at the chosen distance.

If you install hinges at the bottom of a free-standing trellis, and hook-and-eye connectors at the top, you can swing the trellis down and away from the wall, vine and all, whenever you need to repaint the house. This works only with flexible vines, not those with rigid stems, like wisteria. Or you can make the trellis an independent structure of its own, supported on posts sunk into the ground. In this case, make sure to use rot-resistant wood or to soak the post ends in nontoxic wood preservative, and sink the posts deep enough into the ground to withstand the frost in your area—at least 2 feet, but 3 feet where frost is particularly heavy.

PLANTING

PERENNIAL VINES ARE GENERALLY sold as bare-rooted nursery plants and should be planted while they are still dormant, early in the spring. Container-grown plants can be planted at any time, though preferably in the spring as well so that they have a growing season to become established before the winter sets in. Mail-order houses generally ship

Vines screen one area of the garden from another while allowing light and air to pass through.

one- or two-year-old plants with some sort of guarantee.

Annual vines are grown from seeds, which can be planted in the garden whenever danger of frost has passed. To get a head start on their annuals, however, many gardeners start their seeds indoors a month to six weeks before the last frost is due, and as much as eight weeks for slow starters like morning glories. To hasten the germination of morning glories and moon-flowers, which have tough seed coats, soak the seeds overnight in warm water to soften the coats or nick their outer casings with a file.

You can start your seeds in flats or pots filled

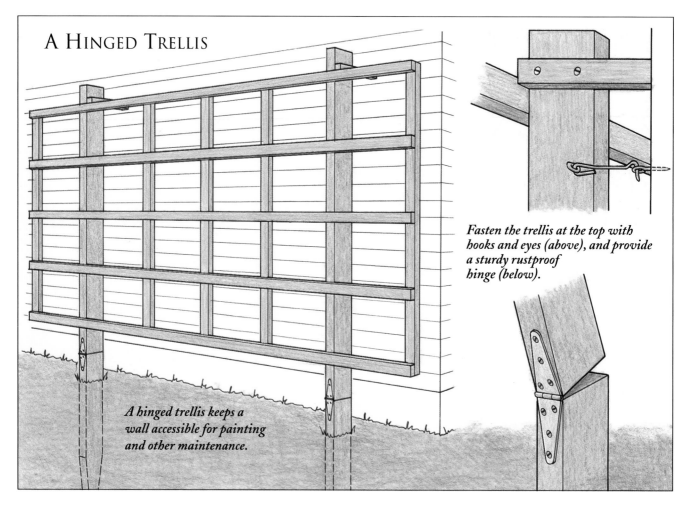

A HINGED TRELLIS

Fasten the trellis at the top with hooks and eyes (above), and provide a sturdy rustproof hinge (below).

A hinged trellis keeps a wall accessible for painting and other maintenance.

with a light mixture of peat moss and potting soil, or use expandable peat pellets. Simply place the pellets in a tray of water, where they will absorb water and expand to several times their original height. Poke three holes in the top of each pellet, insert a seed in each to the prescribed depth and pinch the peat to cover it. Set the tray in a warm spot out of direct sunlight and cover with a clear plastic bag to keep things moist. When the seeds have sprouted, remove the plastic and set the tray in a sunny window, rotating the seedlings occasionally so they don't develop an excessive lean toward the light. When the seedlings begin to crowd one another, snip off all but the largest one in each pellet. To "harden" them up, set them outside for a few hours each day when the weather gets nice, then plant them in the ground.

MOST VINES WILL GROW WELL in the slightly acid soil common around North America (6.5 to 7 on the pH scale). Boston ivy prefers more acid conditions, while clematis takes to more alkaline soil. Before planting, test the soil of your planting bed with a kit purchased at a garden center, or give a sample of soil to the local agricultural extension service, which will tell you how your soil rates. To lower the pH ½ to 1 point, making it slightly more acid, mix in finely ground sulfur at ½ pound per 100 square feet of planting area. To raise the pH 1 point, making the soil more alkaline, mix in 5 pounds of ground limestone per 100 square feet. In both cases, do it a month or two before planting to give the chemicals time to go to work. If you want to lower the pH faster, mix in 3 pounds of iron sulfate per

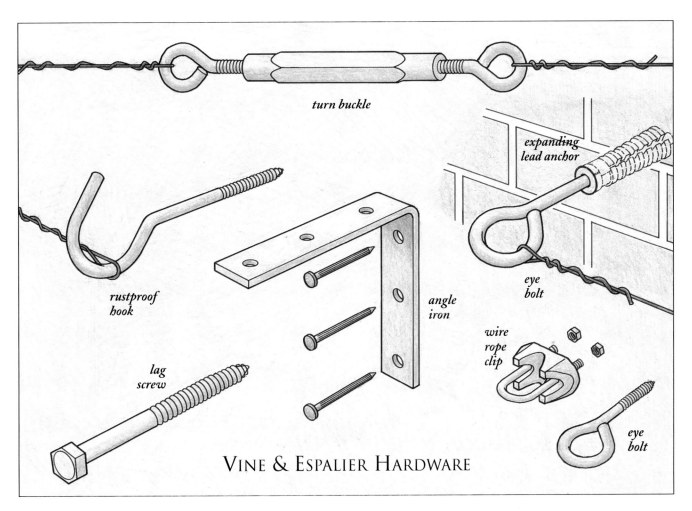

turn buckle

expanding lead anchor

rustproof hook

lag screw

angle iron

eye bolt

wire rope clip

eye bolt

VINE & ESPALIER HARDWARE

100 square feet (iron sulfate leaches away faster than sulfur and may have to be replenished every two years). If your soil is extremely acid or alkaline, or composed of rock-hard clay, it may be simpler to rise above it by growing your vines in tubs, raised plant beds or wooden planters filled with a good commercial soil mix and equipped with holes for drainage.

All vines, annual and perennial, appreciate a soil that retains moisture yet drains well, which means mixing in a generous amount of leaf mold, compost or peat moss. In planting a bare-root or container-grown vine, dig down to a depth of at least 2 feet—more in the case of deep-rooted vines like wisteria—placing the topsoil and subsoil in separate piles. Mix into each pile 1 part organic matter to 2 parts soil, and start to fill the hole with the topsoil mix.

Place the vine at the same depth it was growing at the nursery (clematis should be set 2 or 3 inches lower) and firm the soil around it. In the case of a large vine, fill the hole about two-thirds full of soil, water it, then continue filling with soil to the top. Make a "saucer" of dirt—a dike 2 or three inches high—around the plant and water it thoroughly again. Mulch the ground with 2 inches of ground bark, straw or compost to retain moisture, keeping the mulch from touching the stems.

Most vines are content in regular soil and do not need fertilizer, but you can encourage sturdy root growth and better flowers by feeding them in the spring. A few vines, like silver fleece vine and sweet autumn clematis, will thrive on a second feeding in midsummer. Make sure to use a low-nitrogen formula like bone meal, 5-10-5 or 0-10-10 unless you want a mass of leaves to cover an area quickly, or unless your ivy looks anemic. Scratch it into the soil around the plants and water it in.

TRAINING VINES

A S SOON AS YOU CAN, begin training a vine to its support. Remove any broken, dead or diseased stems and any suckers—fast-growing shoots that grow upright from the shrub's roots—that may pop up. Tie the vine in place loosely, to avoid disrupting the flow of sap as the stems enlarge, using soft garden twine or raffia looped in a figure 8. If the plant came bare-rooted, trim away about one-third of the top growth to compensate for roots cut off when the plant was dug, unless the nursery has already done so. Otherwise, the new roots will be overwhelmed by a too-large plant. Pinch off stem tips just above buds to promote branching and denser growth near the base. As the vine grows dense, an occasional hosing will remove grime and insects. This is best done in the morning so that leaves do not remain wet at night, encouraging mildew and fungal diseases. Water deeply every week or 10 days in dry weather.

As for pruning, most perennial vines need it once a year. Since pruning needs vary by species, make sure to know the habits of your plant before beginning. In northern areas, it is generally best to trim back a woody vine—a vine whose main stem is rigid and remains through the winter—in late winter or early spring, before new growth starts, so that the new growth will have time to mature before the next winter sets in. This is the case with Henry's honeysuckle and silver lace vine, which bloom in late summer or autumn from buds formed on current growth. Wisteria, however, another woody vine, blooms in spring from buds formed the previous summer and should be pruned after it flowers.

Nonwoody vines, which die down in winter and sprout fresh growth each spring, can have their dead stems cut to within a few inches of the ground after cold weather has set in. Whether or not a vine's top growth will live through a winter is somewhat of a guessing game, however: clematis and Boston ivy, for example, may look dead yet come back to life in spring. When in doubt, it is best to leave the old stems in place. They can always be removed if they fail to sprout. Woody vines grown near the limits of their hardiness zones may be protected from winter cold by bringing in soil—or a mulch of hay, straw or evergreen boughs—and mounding it 6 inches to a foot high around the bases of the plants.

Most perennial vines can be propagated from softwood cuttings taken in late spring or early summer. Snip off growing tips about 6 inches long, ¼ inch below the leaf nodes, and remove any flowers or flower buds. Dip the bottom inch of the cutting in a hormone rooting powder sold at garden stores. As a rooting medium, use a 4-inch layer of coarse sand or peat moss, or equal parts of both, or perlite, vermiculite or finely ground sphagnum moss. Make holes 2 inches deep with a pencil, insert the cuttings in the medium and firm it around the stems. Form a miniature greenhouse over the cuttings with clear plastic propped up on sticks and set it in a warm place out of direct sunlight.

When the cuttings have rooted and put out new leaves—from two to three weeks for quick rooters to as long as three months for slower ones—transfer them to individual pots filled with potting soil. In warmer climates, cuttings can be replanted in the garden at any time. In colder areas, they may have to be overwintered in a greenhouse, cold frame or sunny windowsill and set outside when all danger of frost has passed.

Wisteria blooms from buds formed the previous summer, and is pruned after it flowers.

VINES

SELECTED SPECIES OF VINES
ANNUAL VINES

Asarina spp.
(creeping gloxinia, climbing snapdragon)
Height 6 to 10 feet.
Full sun.
Moist, well-drained soil.
Zones 5-8 (perennial in zones 9-10)
Features: Delicate stems with arrow-shaped leaves twine around thin vertical supports. *A. antirrhiniflora* produces 1-inch long, red and yellow, snapdragonlike flowers. *A. barclaiana*, also called *Maurandya barclaiana* (maurandia) bears numerous 3-inch flower trumpets that are pink to deep purple. *A. erubescens*, also known as *Maurandya erubescens*, features rose-pink blooms that are 3 inches or longer.
Planting and care: Start seeds indoors six to eight weeks before the last expected frost, and move the seedlings to the garden when all danger of frost is past. Set plants 1 foot apart at the base of wires or a trellis. Vines will blossom until fall frost. Remove dead flowers and seed pods.

Cardiospermum halicacabum
(balloon vine, love-in-a-puff)
Height 10 feet or more.
Full sun.
Well-drained soil.
Zones 4-8 (perennial in Zones 9-10)
Features: Tiny white flowers are transformed into relatively large, papery, balloon-like seed pods that bob in the breeze. Each pod holds three black seeds marked with a heart-shaped white spot from which the genus takes its Latin name

Above: Cardiospermum halicacabum **(balloon vine)**
Left: Lathyrus odoratus **(sweet pea)**

(save the seeds for next year). The vine, which has finely cut foliage, climbs by means of twining tendrils.
Planting and care: Sow seeds indoors four to six weeks before the last frost, filing them lightly and soaking them overnight to speed germination. Or start seeds outdoors after danger of frost. Set plants 12 to 18 inches apart and provide supports for climbing.

Cobaea scandens
(cup-and-saucer vine, cathedral bells)
Height 15 to 25 feet.
Full sun.
Moist, well-drained soil.
Zones 3-8 (perennial in zones 9-10)
Features: A rampant vine that climbs by means of long tendrils, the vine gets its name from its 2-inch flowers, which resemble upside-down cups and saucers. The flowers open a pale green, turn lilac and then purple with white stripes.
Planting and care: Sow seeds indoors six to eight weeks before the last frost is expected. Once the danger of frost is past, space the seedlings 18 to 24 inches apart and give them a support to climb. Pinch back tips to stimulate branching and flowering.

Dolichos lablab
(hyacinth bean)
Height to 30 feet.
Sun.
Well-drained soil.
Zones 3-8 (perennial in Zones 9-10).
Features: Neither a hyacinth nor a bean, this species grows quickly to cover a fence or trellis, bearing 6-inch leaves and purple or white flowers 2 to 4 inches wide on

Ipomoea alba (moonflower)

long spikes in midsummer, followed by flat, seed-filled pods.

Planting and care: Sow seeds directly in the garden about 1 foot apart when night temperatures remain above 50 degrees F. For earlier blossoming in Zones 3-5, start seeds indoors six to eight weeks before the last frost is due. In Zones 3 and 4, hyacinth bean may need a sheltered location. Provide string or wire supports, or a trellis, for the vine to climb.

Eccremocarpus scaber
(Chilean glory flower)
Height to 10 feet.
Sun.
Moist, well-drained soil.
Zones 3-10
Features: The orange-scarlet flowers, borne the whole summer, are widely lobed and grow in clusters 6 inches long. Shaped like inch-long, open-mouthed goldfish, they are stunning and

long-lasting in flower arrangements. The leaves are soft green and deeply notched.

Planting and care: Start seeds indoors eight weeks before the last expected frost. Set plants outdoors in well-fertilized soil about a foot apart. Vines may reach 10 feet before heavy frost kills them.

Ipomoea alba
(moonflower)
Height to 40 feet.
Sun or partial shade.
Well-drained soil.
Zones 3-10
Features: Fragrant white flowers up to 6 inches across open after sunset from midsummer to frost. The heart-shaped leaves, up to 8 inches across, form a dense screen.

Planting and care: Soak the seeds overnight to soften the tough outer casing, then plant them indoors about six to eight weeks before the last frost. Seeds can also be sown outdoors directly in the ground after any danger of frost has passed. Guide the vines up supports set about a foot apart.

Ipomoea purpurea
(morning glory)
Height to 10 feet.
Sun or partial shade.
Well-drained soil.
Zones 3-10
Features: The most popular vines in America, as spectacular as they are reliable, morning glories form dense masses of heart-shaped, 5-inch leaves and

flowers up to 5 inches across. The *Ipomoea tricolor* variety 'Pearly Gates' has white blossoms, 'Heavenly Blue' bright sky-blue flowers, 'Scarlet O'Hara' deep red blooms. 'Early Call' may be blue, rose or mixed. The flowers of all varieties open in the morning but close by noon.

Planting and care: Sow seeds indoors eight weeks before the last frost, soaking them overnight to soften the tough outer casing, or sow them directly in the garden after any danger of frost has passed. Set plants about a foot apart and provide wires, strings or latticework for them to climb up and around.

Ipomoea quamoclit
(cypress vine)
Height to 20 feet.
Sun or partial shade.
Well-drained soil.
Zones 3-10.
Features: Dark green, fernlike foliage provides a fine back-

Ipomoea quamoclit
(cypress vine)

Ipomoea purpurea (morning glory)

ground for 1½-inch scarlet flowers, which bloom all summer. They open only in the early morning or evening, never in full sun.

Planting and care: Sow seeds indoors four weeks before the last frost, soaking them overnight to soften the tough outer casing, or sow them directly in the ground after the danger of frost has passed (cypress vine is very sensitive to cold, so be careful). Vines should be set 6 to 8 inches apart in rich soil.

Lagenaria spp.
(bottle gourd)
Height to 30 feet.
Sun.
Most soils.
Zones 3-10
Features: Fun for children of all ages, these vines produce highly durable, beige-colored gourds that can be made into birdhouses and birdfeeders, or carved and painted to one's fancy. Another option is to simply wax them with any floor paste wax and use them as centerpieces, parts of

displays, or as an element in any indoor decoration.

Planting and care: Sow the seeds indoors in individual pots about a month before the last danger of frost. When the garden warms up, transplant the seedlings to a sunny, sheltered spot and place them about a foot apart. Let the gourds ripen on the vine, or pick them when almost ripe and let them dry indoors. Wash in a weak solution of household bleach and water to eliminate any mold on the skin.

Tropaeolum majus (common nasturtium)

Lathyrus odoratus
(sweet pea)
Height to 6 feet.
Full sun.
Moist, rich soil.
Zones 3-9.
Features: Sweet peas produce showy, fragrant flowers throughout the summer in colors ranging from pink and red to lavender and blue.
Planting and care: In the South, sweet peas may be planted in fall for late winter blooms. In northern zones, start the seeds indoors in early spring before the last frost, or sow them directly in the soil when danger of frost is past. Soak seeds overnight and dust them with a nitrogen-fixing powder. Sweet peas prefer deep, rich, organic soil. Some perfectionists sow them 6 inches apart at the bottom of a 2-foot trench and cover them with 2 inches of soil, placing well-rotted manure around them as the seedlings grow, until the trench is filled. When plants are 4 inches tall, pinch out the growing tips for side branching. Provide them with netting or chicken wire for support. Remove spent flowers to encourage more blooms.

Phaseolus coccineus
(scarlet runner bean)
Height to 15 feet.
Full sun.
Rich, well-drained soil.
Zones 3-8 (perennial in Zones 9-10)

Features: Scarlet runner bean produces brilliant red flowers that last through summer, as well as edible green beans. It provides a quick cover for fences and trellises.
Planting and care: Plant seeds outdoors in early spring about a foot apart and 2 inches deep in a sunny spot sheltered from wind.

Thunbergia alata
(black-eyed Susan vine)

Tie the growing plants to wires, trellises or other supports until the vines become established and start grasping the support on their own.

Thunbergia alata
(black-eyed Susan vine, clock vine)
Height to 10 feet.
Full sun.
Moist, well-drained soil.
Zones 3-9 (perennial in Zone 10).
Features: Black-eyed Susan vines are notable for their profuse

production of 1-to-2-inch-wide flowers with dark centers and yellow, orange, buff or white petals, which resemble the wildflower black-eyed Susan or daisies from a distance. The leaves are triangle-shaped, 1 to 3 inches long and form a wonderfully dense, green summertime screen.
Planting and care: Sow seeds indoors six to eight weeks before the last spring frost, or directly in the ground after danger of frost has passed. Set plants about 6 inches apart and provide climbing support.

Tropaeolum majus
(common nasturtium)
Height to 10 feet.
Full sun.
Dry, sandy soil.
Zones 3-10.
Features: Nasturtiums produce gaudy displays of 2-inch-wide, funnel-shaped flowers that may be yellow, orange, salmon, pink, scarlet or white. The tartly fragrant blossoms and young lily pad-like leaves are edible and add a peppery flavor to salads or cold soups. Nasturtiums are also long-lasting cut flowers.
Planting and care: Seeds can be sown indoors about a month before the last frost, but since they do not transplant well, and grow quickly, it is easier to sow them directly outdoors when danger of frost has passed. Set them about a foot apart at the base of vertical wires, strings or latticework.

PERENNIAL VINES

Actinidia polygama
(silver vine)
Height to 15 feet.
Sun or partial shade.
Moist, well-drained soil.
Zones 5-10.
Features: The silvery sheen of the male plant's young, heart-shaped leaves gives this vine its common name. The bright green mature leaves are 3 to 5 inches long, sometimes splotched with yellow. Cats seem to be fascinated by the vine, and sometimes claw it to shreds. Male and female flowers are borne on separate plants, so vines of both sexes must be grown to ensure pollination.
Varieties: Also worthy of consideration are *A. arguta* (bower actinidia or tara vine, Zones 5-10), a rampant grower; *A. chinensis* (Chinese gooseberry or kiwi berry, Zones 7-10), grown for its tart-sweet kiwi fruit; and *A. kolomikta* (Kolomikta actinidia, Zones 5-10), a highly ornamental vine with white and pink coloration.
Planting and care: Plant container-grown plants about 2 feet apart. Cut vines back about a third in fall to promote flowering the following year.

Akebia quinata
(five-leaf akebia)
Height 30 feet. or more.
Sun or partial shade.
Well-drained soil.
Zones 4-9.

Features: A fast-growing vine, five-leaf akebia can climb 15 feet in a year. The foliage stays green all year from Zone 7 south, and in northern areas remains on the plant well into the winter but may turn brown. In spring, vines bear clusters of small, fragrant flowers, the females 1 inch wide and purplish brown, the males smaller and light purple.
Planting and care: Plant about 2 feet apart, and provide a strong support such as a sturdy wooden trellis for climbing. Fertilize once a year in spring. Prune after spring flowering to keep plants within bounds. Older plants can be cut back to the ground and will quickly grow back.

Ampelopsis brevipedunculata
(porcelain ampelopsis, porcelain berry)
Height 20 feet or more.
Sun or partial shade.
Light soil.
Zones 4-9.
Features: The most intriguing feature of this vine is its clusters of small berries that ripen in late summer and fall before the vine loses its leaves. The berries are light green to turquoise, lavender, deep purple and porcelain blue—all colors often appearing at the same time. The deeply lobed foliage creates pleasing patterns on an arbor or a wall. Tendrils allow the vine to climb rapidly, up to 15 feet or more in a year.

Varieties: 'Elegans', a slower grower, has leaves beautifully variegated with white and pink.
Planting and care: Plant about 2 feet apart. Prune in spring to thin and shape vines. Fertilize once a year.

Aristolochia durior **(Dutchman's pipe)**
Climbing Rose **(Rosa spp.),** *left*

Aristolochia durior
(Dutchman's pipe)
Height to 30 feet.
Sun or partial shade.
Well-drained soil.
Zones 4-8.
Features: Huge, heart-shaped leaves up to 12 inches long overlap to create a dense screen. Dutchman's pipe, named for its inconspicuous, 1½-inch purplish-brown flowers, which resemble meerschaum pipes, was a popular shade for Victorian homes. A vigorous grower that tolerates urban conditions, it can climb 20

feet in a season, and thus is useful in providing instant privacy or screening out an objectionable view.

Planting and care: Plant about 2 feet apart. Provide stout growing supports. Pinch back stems once or twice a growing season to encourage branching. If the vine threatens to overwhelm you, cut it back to the ground in winter. It will sprout again as vigorously as ever in spring.

Bignonia capreolata (**crossvine**)

Bignonia capreolata
(**crossvine**)
Height to 30 feet or more.
Sun or partial shade.
Well-drained soil.
Zones 7-9.
Features: The crossvine is a rampant grower that puts forth clusters of yellow to brownish-orange, trumpet-shaped flowers in late spring and early summer. They are followed by flat 5-to-7-inch seed pods in fall.
Planting and care: Plant 1 to 3

feet apart. In early spring, prune 3 to 10 feet from each branch to promote new growth and flowers.

Campsis radicans
(**trumpet creeper, trumpet vine**)
Height to 30 feet.
Full sun.
Moist, well-drained soil.
Zones 4-9.
Features: This deciduous vine is covered with spectacular clusters of orange-red, trumpet-shaped blossoms from midsummer through autumn. They are a great favorite of ruby-throated hummingbirds.
Varieties: 'Crimson Trumpet' bears brilliant red flowers. 'Flava' has yellow blossoms. *C. tagliabuana* 'Madame Galen' has pinkish orange flowers and is a hardy choice for northern gardens.
Planting and care: Plant about 2 feet apart. Mulch to keep the soil moist. Tie new vines to supports until their aerial rootlets appear (heavy, mature vines may also need tying). Since trumpet vines flower on the current season's growth, prune in early spring.

Celastrus spp.
(**bittersweet**)
Height 20 to 30 feet.
Sun or partial shade.
Most soils.
Zones 3-8.
Features: *C. orbiculatus* (Oriental bittersweet) and *C. scandens* (American bittersweet) are vigorous ornamental vines. The American species is hardier than its cousin, which cannot be

grown north of Zone 5. On female plants, yellow-orange fruit capsules burst open to reveal scarlet berries, which remain on the vines through winter or until eaten by birds (berry-laden branches, gathered before frost and dried, provide colorful decorations indoors). Green leaves provide good cover until fall, when they turn yellow and drop.
Planting and care: Plant 1 to 2 feet apart. Bittersweet berries are borne only by female plants, which must be pollinated to produce fruit. So make sure you buy at least one male plant (most nurseries label plants by sex). Prune sharply in early spring to keep plants within bounds and to promote fruiting. Bittersweet vines spread by means of underground shoots that may produce new vines where they are not wanted; cut any such offshoots with a sharp spade.

Clematis spp.
(**clematis**)
Height 6 to 30 feet.
Partial shade (full sun in North).
Moist, well-drained, slightly alkaline soil.
Zones 3-9.
Features: No vines surpass clematis for sheer variety of flower shapes and colors. The blossoms, which range from 1 to 10 inches across, have no true petals but 4 to 8 brightly colored, petallike sepals. They are long lasting as cut flowers, and the fluffy seed pods of some species can be used in dried arrangements. All parts of clematis are

Clematis ranunculanaceae 'General Sikorski' (Clematis)

poisonous if eaten.

Varieties: Among some 200 varieties, *C. armandii* (Armand clematis, Zone 7) bears clusters of fragrant, 2½-inch starlike white flowers in late spring. *C. jackmanii* (Jackman clematis, Zone 5) produces deep violet flowers, 4 to 6 inches wide, from summer to fall. *C. montana* 'Rubens' (pink anemone clematis, Zone 5) blooms in spring and summer, bearing rosy clusters of 2-inch, anemone-like flowers. *C. texensis* (scarlet clematis, Zone 4)

bears 1-inch red flowers in summer. *C. tangutica* (golden clematis, Zone 3) has yellow flowers 3 to 4 inches wide from summer to autumn. *C. paniculata* (sweet autumn clematis, Zone 5) puts forth billowy masses of fragrant, creamy-white 1-inch flowers in late summer and fall.

Planting and care: Buy two-year-old plants and set them 2 inches lower in the soil than they were growing in the nursery. Mulch to keep the roots cool. Vines need only occasional pruning. Early-

flowering types like *C. armandii*, which produce blossoms from the previous season's ripened stems, should be pruned after flowering to allow new growth. All others, which produce flowers on the current season's stems, should be pruned in early spring before new growth starts.

Euonymus fortunei
(wintercreeper)
Height to 10 feet or more.
Sun or partial shade.
Moist, well-drained soil.

Hedera helix (English ivy)

Zones 4-9.

Features: Better known as a ground cover than a climber, this species will nevertheless ascend walls or other supports when it comes into contact with them. Its 1-inch oval leaves remain green through the winter.

Varieties: The name 'Erecta' is often applied to climbing types. 'Carrierei' clings well to walls. 'Colorata' has 1-to-2-inch leaves that turn purple or red in fall and winter. Among the types with variegated leaves are 'Uncinata', 'Sunspot', 'Variegata' and 'Gracilis'.

Planting and care: Plant 1 to 2 feet apart. Mulch with ground bark or wood chips to discourage weeds. Provide support such as a wooden trellis or a wall.

Gelsemium sempervirens **(Carolina jasmine, evening trumpet flower)**
Height to 20 feet.
Sun or partial shade.
Rich, well-drained soil.
Zones 7-9.

Features: From late winter through spring, clusters of 1-to-1½-inch yellow, trumpet-shaped flowers fill the air with fragrance. Airy, delicate foliage makes a good light screen. All parts of the plants are poisonous.

Varieties: 'Pride of Augusta' is a beautiful cultivar with double flowers.

Planting and care: Plant 1 to 2 feet apart. Carolina jasmine grows best when its roots are shaded and cool. Apply a balanced fertilizer while the plant is actively growing. Prune immediately after flowering, removing dead or broken branches and shaping the vine.

Hedera helix
(English ivy)
Height to 50 feet or more.
Shade to partial sun.
Well-drained soil.
Zones 4-9.
Features: A much-loved plant brought from Europe by early Colonists, English ivy is a perennial favorite for covering sheltered and shady walls. Its small black berries are poisonous if eaten.
Varieties: Of the scores of named varieties of English ivy, 'Baltica' is the hardiest (Zone 4) and one of the most tolerant of sun; it has white-veined leaves 1 to 2 inches across. 'Bulgaria' is also hardy (Zone 5) and has large leaves 4 to 5 inches wide. '238th Street', named for the location of a churchyard in New York City where it was found, is another hardy choice (Zone 5), with 1½-inch heart-shaped leaves veined with yellow. In northern gardens, English ivy tends to turn brown from sun and wind during the winter.
Planting and care: Plant 1 foot apart in loam enriched with compost, peat moss or leaf mold. Mulch for weed control, and water deeply during periods of drought. Prune in spring to maintain the desired size and shape.

Hydrangea anomala petiolaris
(climbing hydrangea)
Height to 50 feet.
Sun or partial shade.
Moist, well-drained soil.
Zones 5-7.
Features: A deciduous vine notable for its oval leaves and large, lovely white flower clusters.
Planting and care: Plant individually in garden soil enriched with organic matter. Fertilize each spring with a balanced fertilizer

Hydrangea anomala petiolaris
(climbing hydrangea)

such as one marked 5-10-5. Mulch in fall for winter protection. Prune in winter or early spring to maintain the desired shape. The vine gets off to a slow start, but after two or three years becomes a vigorous climber.

Jasminium nudiflorum
(winter jasmine)
Height to 15 feet.
Sun.
Well-drained soil.

Zones 5-10.
Features: The hardiest of the jasmines, this species can be grown as far north as Boston when given some protection; in the South it remains evergreen and blooms in winter. It produces bright yellow, solitary 1-inch flowers that are very fragrant.
Planting and care: Plant 1 to 2 feet apart in a warm, dry, sunny location for maximum flowering. Prune occasionally to prevent the plant from becoming untidy. Flower buds can be forced into bloom indoors in the winter.

Lonicera spp.
(honeysuckle)
Height 15 feet or more.
Sun or partial shade.
Rich, well-drained soil.
Zones 4-9.
Features: Fast-growing vines, honeysuckles produce abundant tubular flowers in shades of yellow, white, red, orange or coral. Birds relish the seeds.
Varieties: *L. japonica* 'Halliana' (Hall's honeysuckle), one of the most widely grown varieties, has highly fragrant white flowers; it quickly produces a dense tangle of stems that may grow 15 feet in a season and that root wherever they touch the ground. Evergreen in mild climates, its leaves turn bronze in cold areas before dropping in late fall. Less rampant is *L. henryi* (Henry's honeysuckle), which bears yellowish or reddish purple flowers. *L. sempervirens* (trumpet or

coral honeysuckle) has scentless coral or red flowers followed by red berries and is hardy to Zone 4. *L.* x *brownii* 'Dropmore Scarlet', with bright red blossoms, flourishes even in Zone 3. *L. heckrotti* (everblooming honeysuckle) bears fragrant pink flowers from late spring to fall.

Planting and care: Plant about 2 feet apart. Prune after flowering to maintain the desired size and

Parthenocissus tricuspidata
(Boston ivy)

shape. Remove some of the old stems each year to promote new growth from the base.

Menispermum canadense
(moonseed)
Height to 15 feet.
Sun or shade.
Tolerates wet, poor soil.
Zones 5-8.
Features: A fast-growing vine with large, ivylike leaves up to 8 inches across. Inconspicuous greenish-white flowers bloom all

summer and are followed by clusters of poisonous black berries. The vines remain evergreen in mild climates but die back to the ground in the North.
Planting and care: Plant about 1 to 2 feet apart. The vine spreads rapidly by means of underground runners and can become invasive if not kept under close control. Moonseed is one of the few vines that will flourish in a shady, wet, poor soil and needs no protection from the wind.

Parthenocissus quinquefolia
(Virginia creeper, woodbine)
Height to 20 feet or more.
Sun or partial shade.
Most soils.
Zones 3-9.
Features: The vigorous, high-climbing Virginia creeper is valued for its graceful clusters of five leaves, which turn a vivid scarlet in autumn, especially in sun. Poisonous, shiny, dark blue berries appear before the leaves drop, exposing a delicate tracery of woody stems. Attractive to birds, Virginia creeper tolerates urban conditions.
Varieties: 'Engelmannii' has smaller, leathery leaves. 'Saint Paulii' clings well to stone and other rough surfaces.
Planting and care: Plant 3 to 4 feet apart. Young vines need to be guided to the supports on which they will grow.

Parthenocissus tricuspidata
(Boston ivy)
Height to 60 feet.
Sun or partial shade.

Most soils (slightly acid).
Zones 4-8.
Features: Sometimes called Japanese creeper, this Oriental vine is widely used to blanket public buildings in cooler regions where English ivy is not hardy (it grows much faster). Its shiny green leaves, up to 8 inches across, look somewhat like maple leaves and turn reddish orange in fall. All parts of Boston ivy are poisonous.
Planting and care: Plant 1 to 2 feet apart. Prefers sun, a rich soil and good air circulation, but will tolerate shade, dry conditions and air pollution.

Passiflora spp.
(passionflower)
Height to 20 feet or more.
Sun.
Deep, moist soil.
Zones 7-10.
Features: Passionflowers bear spectacular blossoms up to 5 inches across from late spring to early fall, depending on the species. The attractive foliage is evergreen, though some species lose their leaves in cooler regions.
Varieties: *P. alatocaerulea* (hybrid passionflower) produces purple, blue, pink and white blooms 4 inches wide. *P. caerulea* (blue passionflower) has similar flowers 3 to 4 inches across. *P. coccinea* (red passionflower) has 3-to-5-inch scarlet flowers, the vivid petals and sepals surrounding a purple, pink and white crown.
Planting and care: Plant about 1 foot apart in full sun in a well-drained soil enriched with

Parthenocissus quinquefolia (Virginia creeper)

Passiflora spp. (passionflower)

compost or leaf mold. Prune
vines heavily in fall or early
spring to remove deadwood and
control rampant growth.

Polygonum aubertii
(silver lace vine)
Height 25 feet or more.
Sun or partial shade.
Most soils.
Zones 4-8.
Features: Also dubbed "mile-a-
minute vine," this species can
twine to 25 feet or more during a
single growing season. In late
summer and early fall, it is
covered with 6-inch clusters of
small, fragrant white blossoms,
adding a welcome floral display
at this time of year.
Planting and care: Plant about
1 to 2 feet apart. Tie the
branches to strong supports (it
is a good choice to cover a
chain-link fence). The vine
flowers on new wood and
should be cut back drastically in
fall or winter.

Rosa spp.
(climbing roses)
Height to 20 feet.
Sun.
Well-drained, composted soil.
Zones 5-9.
Features: For those willing to
take care of them, climbing roses
provide spectacular rewards,
blooming from spring through
fall in shades of white, yellow,
pink and red.
Varieties: Among the many
choices are the large-flowered
climbers, which bear 2-to-6-inch
blossoms early in the season;
some varieties bloom intermit-
tently after that and then burst
forth with another heavy crop in
fall. Rambling roses grow rapidly
and produce dense clusters of
small flowers no more than 2
inches across. Most bloom in late
spring or early summer, and a
few flower again in fall. There
are also climbing versions of
hybrid tea roses, floribundas,
grandifloras, polyanthas and even
miniature roses. Hybrids named
Kordesii bloom profusely all
season long; they are extremely
hardy, requiring no winter
protection as far north as Zone 4.
Among the best large climbing
roses are 'Climbing Peace',
'America', 'Blaze', 'Golden
Showers', 'New Dawn' and
'Viking Queen'.
Planting and care: Plant roses in
the spring, spacing them 5 to 8
feet apart. Because they lack the
tendrils of true vines, they must
be tied to a support such as a
trellis or a fence, preferably in a
fan shape. Water the plants

heavily in dry weather, spread
compost in the fall, and feed
plants in the spring with a
balanced garden fertilizer.
Remove spent flowers to lengthen
the blooming season.
Immediately after flowering,
prune out old or dead canes and
remove inward-growing or
crossing branches. For winter
protection in colder regions,
place canes on the ground and
cover them up with soil.

Vitis spp.
(grape)
Height to 20 feet or more.
Sun.
Most soils.
Zones 4-9.
Features: These fast-growing,
coarse vines make dense mats of
foliage that screen effectively,
and many varieties have the
added dividend of producing
edible grapes.
Varieties: Among the types
grown for their ornamental value
alone are *V. amurensis* (Amur
grape), *V. coignetiae* (crimson
glory vine) and *V. riparia* (river-
bank grape). Edible American
varieties (*V. labrusca*), which
grow as far north as Zone 4,
include 'Catawba', 'Delaware',
'Eastern Concord', 'Fredonia'
and 'Niagara'. Edible European
varieties (*V. vinifera*), which
grow from Zone 7 south, include
'Flame Seedless', 'Perlette', 'Ruby
Seedless', 'Seibel' and 'Thompson
Seedless'.
Planting and care: Plant at least
two vines to assure pollination,
spacing them about 8 feet apart.

Rosa spp. (climbing roses)

They do best in a moist, well-drained, slightly alkaline soil that has been enriched with organic material and covered with a mulch. Grapes need good air circulation to avoid mildew and may need to be treated with a fungicide such as copper sulfate. Apply nitrogen fertilizer to promote foliage growth. For good fruit production, train to one or more horizontal wires set at 2-foot intervals above the ground, pruning the stems back to two leaf buds in winter and tying the resultant branches along the wires.

Wisteria spp.
(wisteria)
Height 25 feet or more.
Full sun.
Well-drained soil.
Zones 4-9.
Features: Pendulous clusters of fragrant flowers a foot or more long are the hallmark of these sturdy spring-blooming deciduous vines. Their stems become woody, twisted trunks with age, adding character and interest. The seeds inside the pods are poisonous.
Varieties: The sweetly scented flower clusters of *W. floribunda* (Japanese wisteria) are 12 to 24 inches long, and the leaves have 13 to 19 leaflets. Among cultivated varieties are 'Alba' (white), 'Rosea' (pink), 'Longissima' (lavender), 'Macrobotrys' (reddish violet) and 'Violacea Plena' (double-flowered purple). The blue-to-violet flower clusters of *W. sinensis* (Chinese wisteria) are

Wisteria spp.

6 to 12 inches long and less fragrant; they bloom all at once before the leaves, composed of 7 to 13 leaflets, appear. 'Alba' and 'Jako' have white flowers.

Planting and care: Set individual plants about a foot from their support—which should be a sturdy one such as a substantial wooden trellis—and tie their branches to the support to start them off. To avoid a long wait, since wisteria is slow-growing, try to find potted vines that have already flowered. Keep the plants well watered, and mulch them during the first winter. To stimulate blooming, feed the plants with bonemeal or another fertilizer high in phosphorus, and prune plants heavily after they flower and again in winter. It is also a good idea to prune the roots in early spring by plunging a spade into the ground in a circle one foot out from the trunk for every inch of trunk diameter. (To determine trunk diameter, hold a ruler alongside and estimate.)

A LIST OF SPECIES BY FUNCTION

Vines for Foliage

Actinidia polygama (silver vine)

Aristolochia durior (Dutchman's pipe)

Clematis spp. (clematis)

Euonymus fortunei (wintercreeper)

Hedera helix (English ivy)

Hydrangea anomala petiolaris (climbing hydrangea)

Ipomoea alba (moonflower)

Ipomoea purpurea (morning glory)

Menispermum canadense (moonseed)

Parthenocissus quinquefolia (Virginia creeper, woodbine)

Parthenocissus tricuspidata (Boston ivy)

Vitis spp. (grape)

Vines for Flowers or Fruits

Ampelopsis brevipedunculata (porcelain berry)

Asarina (creeping gloxinia, climbing snapdragon)

Bignonia capreolata (crossvine)

Campsis radicans (trumpet creeper, trumpet vine)

Cardiospermum halicacabum (balloon vine, love-in-a-puff)

Celastrus spp. (bittersweet)

Clematis spp. (clematis)

Cobaea scandens (cup-and-saucer vine, cathedral bells)

Dolichos lablab (hyacinth bean)

Eccremocarpus scaber (Chilean glory flower)

Gelsemium sempervirens (Carolina jasmine, evening trumpet flower)

Hydrangea anomala petiolaris (climbing hydrangea)

Ipomoea alba (moonflower)

Ipomoea quamoclit (cypress vine)

Ipomoea purpurea (morning glory)

Jasminium nudiflorum (winter jasmine)

Lagenaria spp. (bottle gourd)

Lathyrus odoratus (sweet pea)

Lonicera spp. (honeysuckle)

Passiflora spp. (passionflower)

Phaseolus coccineus (scarlet runner bean)

Polygonum aubertii (silver lace vine)

Rosa spp. (climbing roses)

Thunbergia alata (black-eyed Susan vine, clock vine)

Tropaeolum majus (climbing or common nasturtium)

Wisteria spp. (wisteria)

Fast-growing Vines

Akebia quinata (five-leaf akebia)

Aristolochia durior (Dutchman's pipe)

Bignonia capreolata (crossvine)

Cobaea scandens (cup-and-saucer vine, cathedral bells)

Dolichos lablab (hyacinth bean)

Ipomoea alba (moonflower)

Ipomoea quamoclit (cypress vine)

Ipomoea purpurea (morning glory)

Lonicera spp. (honeysuckle)

Phaseolus coccineus (scarlet runner bean)

Polygonum aubertii (silver lace vine)

Vitis spp. (grape)

CHAPTER THREE

ESPALIERS
FOUR-SEASON FENCES

SPALIERS ARE PLANTS SUCH AS FRUIT TREES OR ornamentals that have been trained on wires or trellises into a variety of patterns. Much like vines, espaliers can be trained against blank walls or fences, or they may act as a freestanding fence when supported by a sturdy post-and-wire framework of their own. Though they require more labor than a vine or a hedge, an espalier will reward the gardener with its foliage and flowers, its decorative pattern and, in many cases, with luscious fruit.

The term espalier, a French word adapted from the old Italian *spallieria* ("something to lean against"), applies to any plant grown in a flat, two-dimensional pattern. Espalier originated in Europe's medieval walled towns, where during long sieges it was necessary to grow fruit in a confined area, such as against the rampart walls. In addition to saving space, the new technique had surprising advantages. It was discovered that sun heat reflected from the wall encouraged the trees to bear fruit earlier than expected, and the two-dimensional pattern improved the size and quality of the fruit by opening up the trees to sunlight and air. By the 18th century,

espaliered fruit trees were widely planted in Europe and England, not only in the formal, geometric gardens of the aristocracy but also in the kitchen yards of ordinary peasants and farmers. In America, espaliers may be seen at George Washington's home in Mount Vernon, at the Tryon Palace, built for the Colonial governor in New Bern, North Carolina, and in the restoration gardens of Williamsburg, Virginia.

Though a finished design may take several years to complete, the advantages of espaliering are many. Espaliered apple trees, for example, bear fruit in two to three years, compared to the seven to eight years required for standard trees. Aside from opening the tree to sunlight, espalier patterns often bend the branches downward toward the horizontal. This slows its growth, and energy is then channeled into the production of bigger flowers and fruit. With espaliers, pruning, spraying and picking fruit is much easier, because everything is within reach without need for a ladder, especially if dwarfed varieties are used. Espaliers take up little space, leaving the ground around them free for other uses. Their patterns are decorative even in winter when the leaves have fallen.

For those impatient for results, some nurseries sell plants already trained into espalier form. These ready-made ones are usually popular varieties like firethorns or dwarf apples and pears. For example, Henry Leuthardt Nurseries in East Moriches, New York, an espalier specialist, offers apples or pears in single vertical cordons 6 to 7 feet tall, in U-form espaliers, and in six-armed candelabra shapes. With a little patience, however, you can train your own espaliers from less expensive 1- or 2-year-old "whips," young trees that do not have side shoots, and have far more species and designs to choose from.

Right: Apple trees in the Belgian fence pattern.
Previous page: Apple trees on a post-and-wire
framework in a two-tiered horizontal T.

A double U-shape espalier livens up the bland surface of a palisade fence while putting what would otherwise have been an unused space to use, producing home-grown pears.

Espaliers can be trained into traditional, formal designs, such as the palmette verrier, in which the tree's branches ascend like the arms of a candelabra, or the palmette oblique, in which the branches are trained to grow at an angle. In the Belgian fence, plants are trained to grow into an overlapping lattice. Another possibility is training the plants into free-form designs. Sometimes a shrub or small tree will have individual characteristics that will lend it to an informal design. It will need only a little pruning and training to grow into a natural and graceful pattern. Among the many species that can be trained into informal fans or fountains because of their natural growth habits are forsythia, quince and yew.

STRUCTURES FOR ESPALIERS

FRUIT-BEARING ESPALIERS need at least six hours of sunlight a day during the growing season in order to blossom and set fruit. As with vines, espaliered plants can be grown directly on walls, and often flower earlier than those planted in the open because of the protection and warmth that the wall affords.

A graceful palmette oblique is this apple tree's pattern. Espaliers can be grown directly on brick or other masonry walls, without need for the extra space that a wooden wall requires to reduce risk of rot.

In most cases, however, especially with wooden walls, it is wise to leave at least 6 inches between espalier and wall to promote air circulation, reduce chances of rot and allow room for tying, pruning and the formation of fruit.

The gap is particularly important if the wall is light-colored and south-facing. So much heat can be reflected from the wall that it will literally cook the plant and any fruit it bears unless you give it breathing room. In such a case, plant the espalier a foot away from the wall to prevent damage from reflected sun, and train it onto a wooden trellis. Built of rot-resistant slats of redwood, cedar or cypress with slats in a grid or diagonal latticework pattern, a trellis has the added advantage of looking permanent, creating the illusion of a completed espalier long before the plant being trained to it reaches maturity. If the trellis is hinged at the bottom, and fastened with hook-and-eye fasteners at the top (see page 66), it can be gently tilted down and away from the wall for painting or other maintenance. The hinged trellis will only work for flexible-stemmed plants like forsythia, but not for rigid, woody trees like apples.

For brick, stone or concrete block walls, you can dispense with a wooden trellis and use horizontal wires instead. Make sure that the

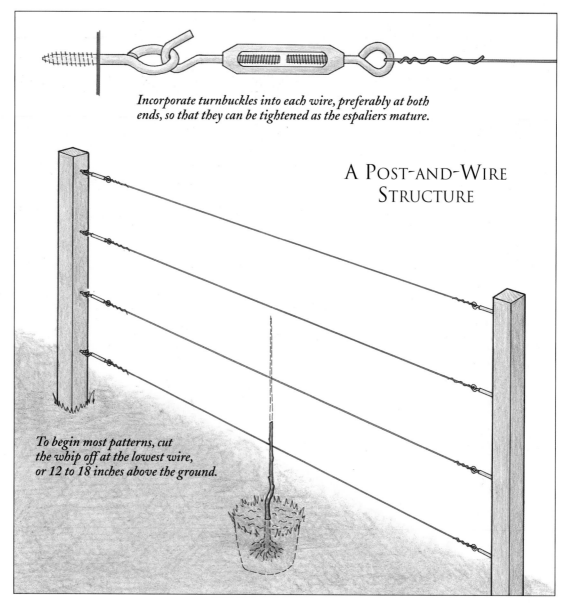

Incorporate turnbuckles into each wire, preferably at both ends, so that they can be tightened as the espaliers mature.

A POST-AND-WIRE STRUCTURE

To begin most patterns, cut the whip off at the lowest wire, or 12 to 18 inches above the ground.

lowest wire is about 18 inches from the ground, and the ones above it about 1 to 2 feet apart. To string one horizontal wire, drill holes with a masonry drill at 3- or 4-foot intervals, and insert into the holes lead expansion shields available at any hardware store. Into the shields screw 5-to-7-inch-long eyebolts or lag screws (see page 67), making sure that they project at least 4 to 6 inches from the wall to permit air circulation behind the espalier. String wire through the eyebolts or around the lag screws and secure it by twisting the end of the wire around its length or by fastening it with a wire rope clip. Number 14 galvanized wire is strong enough to support most espaliers, or you can use number 14 vinyl-coated wire. Continue stringing wires to a height of 5 to 7 feet.

Free-standing espaliers, trained to an independent supporting framework, can also be used to screen one area from another. A vegetable garden can be separated from a formal garden or a work area from an outdoor-living patio by an espalier trained to an existing post-and-rail or chain-link fence.

Several low posts support apples in a two-tiered horizontal T.

These espaliered pears bring greenery and fruit to a quiet corner. In the winter, when the leaves have fallen, their pattern will be visible, providing visual interest in an otherwise blank space.

Or a sturdy framework can be built with wooden 4-by-4-inch posts. The posts should be set 8 to 10 feet apart along the area you want to screen. Use rot-resistant redwood, cypress or cedar, or pressure-treated lumber. Sink the posts at least 2 feet into the ground, 3 feet or more in areas of heavy frost, making sure they are vertical with a carpenter's level. Screw a heavy eye screw into the inside of each post, starting at least 12 inches above the soil line and moving upwards at 12-to-18-inch intervals to a height of 5 to 7 feet. Loop number 14 galvanized or black plastic-coated wire into one eye screw and bring it horizontally across to the eye screw on the opposite post. Before securing it to the next eye screw, make sure that the wire is true with the level. Then hook a 3-inch turnbuckle, opened to its maximum extent, into the eye screw. Loop the end of the wire through the eye in the turnbuckle, on the opposite end. Check again with the level to see that the wire is true, and then double the loose end of the wire back along the strung wire. Fasten it to the strung wire with a wire rope clip, or twist it into place. A turnbuckle should be inserted in every wire strung so that it can be tightened whenever the wire slackens under the weight of the maturing plant.

PLANTING ESPALIERS

FRUIT TREES MAY BE PLANTED in the fall, when the soil is in good condition and the weather is often better. A fall-planted tree will start growing earlier the following spring. In regions with severe winters, however, like northern New England, it is wiser to plant any tree or shrub in the spring. All fruit trees require a dormant period of 45 days, with temperatures of 45 degrees F or less, in order to blossom and set fruit. Apples are the hardiest fruit trees, generally frost-resistant to −25 degrees F. They are followed by pears, cherries, apricots, peaches and nectarines, which can stand temperatures no lower than −12 degrees F. With the exception of peaches, nectarines and apricots, which are self-fruitful, fruit trees should be planted near another member of the same family that blooms at the same time to ensure cross-pollination. To get a full crop, for example, plant two varieties of apple within 40 to 60 feet of one another. 'Cortland', 'Red Delicious', 'Rome Beauty', 'Yellow Delicious' and 'Jonathan' are all good pollinators.

Planting an espalier is much like planting anything else. It should be done in soil well enriched by compost or leaf mold, with the plant's roots spread out. When planting next to a wall, watch out for rubble left as backfill and lime leaching into the soil from concrete foundations, which could turn the soil too alkaline.

If you have any doubts about your soil, test it with a soil testing kit, sold at garden centers, or send soil samples to your county extension agent. Most fruit trees flourish in a neutral to slightly alkaline soil with a pH of 6 to 6.5; camellias and a few others prefer a slightly more acid soil. If your soil is overly acid (pH below 6), you can correct it by adding ground limestone. If it is overly sweet (pH above 7), add leaf mold, peat moss, sulfate of potash or superphosphate.

If the whip you have ordered is bare-root, shipped while dormant with its roots free of soil, soak the roots for one or two hours before planting. If you can't plant right away, make sure the roots are moist in their packing and place the plants in a cool place out of the sun, such as a carport or unheated garage. Should you be unable to plant for several days, "heel" the plants into the ground by digging a trench, laying the plants at an angle in the trench and covering the roots with moist soil.

DIG A GENEROUS HOLE, at least 1½ times the diameter of the roots in all directions, and place the whip in it. The plant should sit at the same level it was growing at the nursery. If the plant is too low in the hole, remove it, mound more soil in the bottom of the hole, and try it again. Once it is at the correct height, gently spread out its roots and fill in around them with topsoil, working the soil with your hands to make sure no air pockets remain. A little 5-10-5 fertilizer, about a pound for every inch of trunk diameter, can be worked in to give the plants a start. To determine trunk diameter, hold a ruler next to the plant and estimate. Take care not to over-fertilize—too-rich soil stimulates foliage growth at the expense of fruit-bearing wood. When the roots are covered, sprinkle on a half-bucket of water to settle the soil. Once the water has drained away, continue filling with soil to the top of the hole, using subsoil if necessary. Tamp down the earth with your foot and water again. Make a saucer—a 2-inch raised dike—of soil around the planting hole to retain water, and mulch with 2 inches of straw, compost, ground bark or leaf mold, keeping the mulch a few inches away from the stem to prevent rot. Water thoroughly the first time, and water again every week to 10 days thereafter if the weather is dry. Generally, 1 inch of water a week provides enough moisture during the growing season.

If you are planting a grafted rootstock, common on dwarf fruit trees, make sure that the

ESPALIER PATTERNS

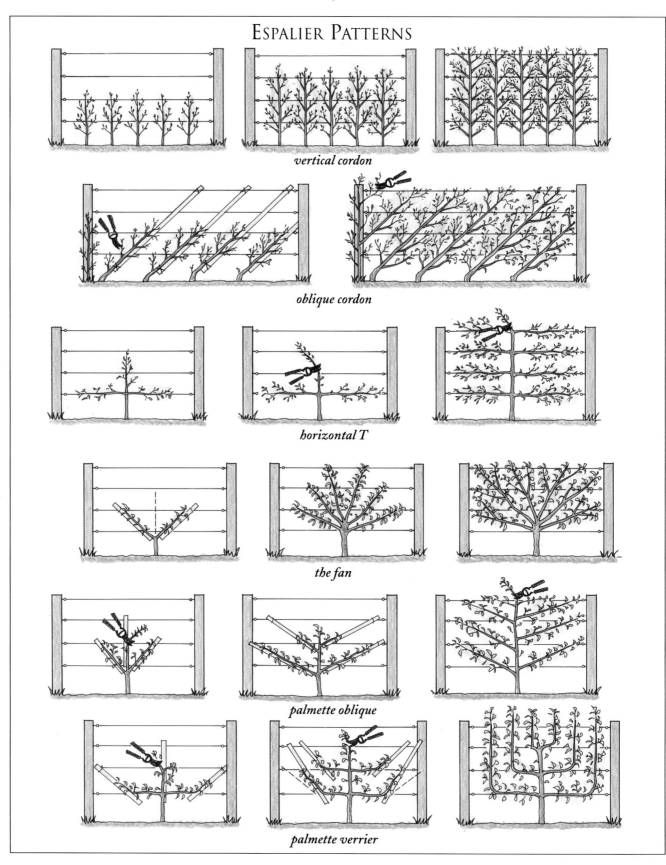

vertical cordon

oblique cordon

horizontal T

the fan

palmette oblique

palmette verrier

knobby graft line, or bud union, is 2 inches above the soil, and keep mulch away from it. If moist soil touches the bud union, the upper part of the tree will send out roots, producing a full-sized tree instead of the dwarf you expected.

WHEN PRUNING GROWING and completed espaliers, bear in mind that a new shoot will form in the same direction that a bud now on the branch is facing, and slant your cut about ¼ inch above a bud and away from it. Pruning should be done at any time during the growing season to remove dead, broken, diseased or crossing branches, as well as any that stick out of the flat pattern or do not otherwise contribute to the design that you have chosen. Apple and pear trees bear fruit on spurs, twiglets less than 6 inches long that produce fat flower buds followed by fruit. Leave spurs alone. Summer pruning, started after the first flush of growth, helps to induce the formation of new spurs. In colder climates, do not prune after the end of August, or you will stimulate new growth that could be killed by early frosts. Once an espalier is completed, it will take periodic pruning to keep its natural growth within bounds.

Winter protection is not needed for most espaliers, though it is wise to cover any plant set against a light-colored, south-facing wall with burlap to prevent damage from reflected heat.

ESPALIER PATTERNS

CHOOSING A PATTERN FOR ESPALIER is a question of both aesthetics and practicality. A thorough discussion of the shapes and patterns most often used in espalier follows. Your choice should reflect what you intend the espalier for, the species used for the espalier, and your abilities and confidence as a gardener.

The simplest espalier, and thus the easiest for beginners, is a **vertical cordon**. A single, up-right plant, the vertical cordon is often planted in a row at intervals of 1 to 3 feet, depending on how dense a screening effect you want. If permitted, vertical cordons will eventually grow together to make a solid screen. The pattern can be used as a decorative treatment against walls, as a freestanding fence, or as a divider between various areas of the garden. On fruit trees, the severely shortened side branches of the vertical cordon become loaded with fruiting buds, making it an effective shape for fruit production.

The growing plants can be trained directly to a trellis, or, if the plant will be trained to horizontal wires on a masonry wall or in a post-and-wire structure, to long vertical bamboo or wooden stakes. If the spaces in your trellis are large, you may want to use stakes to support the young plants as they grow across them. Set the stakes into the ground where you will plant and tie the stakes to the wires with soft twine, plastic tying ribbon, raffia or serrated, slip-on plant ties, all available at garden centers. Wall lath, available at lumber yards, is especially good for stakes. It can be split in two lengthwise, yielding wooden strips 4 feet long and ⅜ by ¾ inches wide. Plant a whip at the base of each stake and tie it to the stake loosely, so as not to constrict the flow of nutrients in the stem. Examine the ties periodically to see if they need loosening. If you find the bare end posts of a post-and-wire structure unsightly and want to obscure them, plant additional vertical cordons at the bases of the posts and train the plants to cover them.

As the plants grow, prune off any side shoots to encourage short, compact growth along the central stem, taking care to leave ample fruiting spurs. When the plants reach the top wire or the top of the trellis, lop off the leader—the top-most, terminal shoot. The plants can then be tied directly to the wires or trellis and the temporary stakes removed. Continue to cut off further growth to keep the pattern intact.

A simple variation on the vertical cordon is the **diagonal or oblique cordon**, in which the plants are trained to grow at a 45-degree angle.

ESPALIER PATTERNS

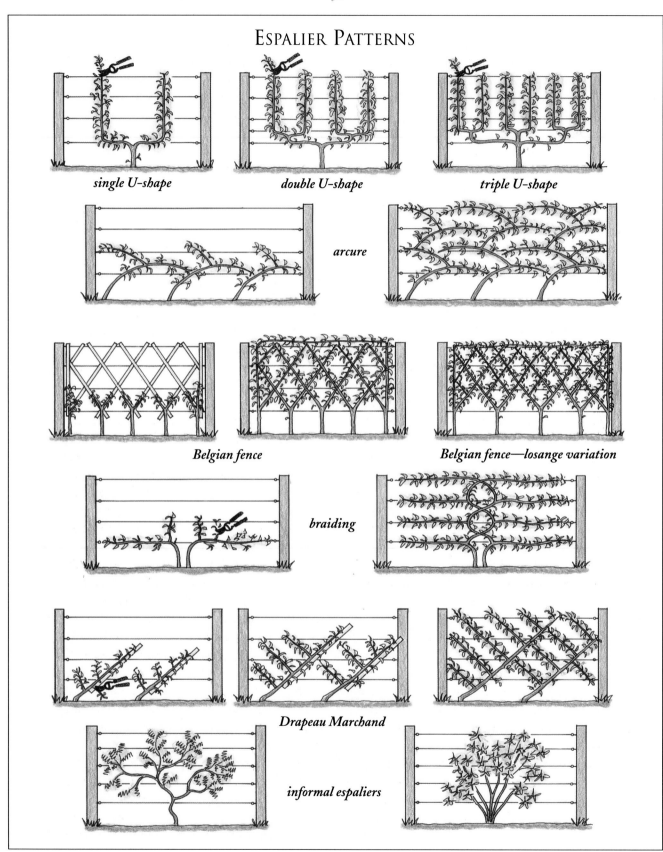

single U-shape

double U-shape

triple U-shape

arcure

Belgian fence

Belgian fence—losange variation

braiding

Drapeau Marchand

informal espaliers

All the whips can be trained in one direction, creating diagonal bars, or alternate plants can be angled in opposite directions so that an overlapping, latticework effect is obtained. As in the vertical cordon, whips should be planted at intervals of 1 to 3 feet, depending on the thickness of screening desired.

It will take few months during the first growing season to bend the stems to a 45-degree angle. Plant the whips normally, and begin to train them by tying stakes to the wires at a 60-degree angle, and then tying the whips to the stakes. Or, if you are training the whips on a trellis, tie them directly to the trellis at a 60-degree angle, using stakes to bridge large gaps, if necessary. As the season progresses and the whips grow, bend and retie the stakes and whips or whips alone, bending them at an ever greater angle, until 45 degrees is reached. If you do not want the end posts of a post-and-wire framework to be seen, plant single vertical cordons in front of them. You may allow selected side shoots to grow into the pattern if you are aiming for a latticework effect, or cut back the side shoots to short, fruit-bearing spurs and keep them at this length to encourage compact growth along the central stem. When the stems are strong enough to stand alone, generally in the second year after planting, remove any stakes and tie the stems directly to the wires or to the trellis. Prune off the leaders, the topmost, terminal shoots, when the desired height is reached.

S LIGHTLY MORE COMPLEX than the vertical and diagonal cordons is the **horizontal T**, in which two branches are trained in opposite directions from a central stem. Set plants for the horizontal T individually, spacing them at least 8 feet apart if you plan on having more than one in a row. To begin, plant a single whip and tie it to a vertical stake to steady it. When the whip is 12 inches long and reaches the lowest wire of the wire framework or the bottom of the trellis, generally in its first year, cut it off at that height. When you cut the whip,

make sure that your cut is above at least three strong-looking buds, and make the cut about ¼ inch above the topmost bud, slanting away from it. Shoots will grow from these buds as the whip concentrates its energy in them rather than in growing upward. Choose the three strongest-looking shoots and prune off the rest. Train two shoots horizontally to the right and left, along the wires or against the trellis, and one shoot straight up a stake or the trellis. This vertical shoot is the leader, or terminal shoot. Prune any offshoots as they appear. If you want only one tier, early the following spring, cut off the leader at or near the first wire, or where the horizontal branches have been trained, and as the new shoots grow, gradually bend them to the horizontal, using stakes if needed, and tie them to the wire or trellis. The end result will look like a single T, a fine design for a low garden border.

I F YOU WANT TWO OR MORE TIERS for your horizontal T, cut the leader at the second wire or 12 to 18 inches above the first horizontal tier early in the spring, before the sap is flowing. Make sure to cut above at least three strong-looking buds, slanting your cut away from the topmost one. As for the first tier, choose the three best shoots that appear and remove the others. Train two shoots horizontally along the wires or the trellis and one vertically. For the third and fourth tiers, repeat the process, cutting the leader at the next wire or 12 to 18 inches above the previous year's tier in the early spring and training the three best shoots. Cut off any watersprouts, long, fast-growing vertical shoots, that form on any of the horizontal branches. A four-tiered horizontal espalier will take four years to grow but will bring you pleasure for many years.

For the horizontal T—or for any other espalier—bend the branches during the growing season, when they are slightly thicker than a pencil and have grown a foot or more beyond the point at which they will be bent. Remove any shoots that don't contribute to the pattern.

If the stems of a plant are tough and woody, you may have to train them to the horizontal in gradual stages. Tie the shoots that will be trained to stakes set at 45 degrees. When they have grown 2 or 3 feet long, bend them down to 30 degrees and retie them. If necessary, add another stage until they are completely horizontal. Or you can modify your horizontal T by leaving the stakes at 45 degrees and training the next side branches at 45 degrees, and so on up the wires or trellis, producing a graceful fan-shape called a palmette oblique.

The **palmette oblique** is similar to the horizontal T, except that its branches ascend on a diagonal. The angle may be 45 degrees for all branches, or it may vary from 30 degrees for the lowest branches to 60 degrees for the highest. As with the horizontal T, set the plants individually, spacing them at least 8 feet apart if you plan on having more than one in a row. The pruning and training is similar to a horizontal T as well. Cut the whip at the first wire on a framework or the bottom of the trellis, making sure to cut above at least three strong-looking buds. When shoots appear, remove all but the best three shoots, shortening any side shoots to spurs. As the shoots grow, tie two to stakes attached diagonally to the wires or tie them diagonally to the trellis, using stakes to bridge large gaps, and train the third, the leader, vertically. The next growing season, prune the leader, and train the three best shoots in the same way, two to diagonal stakes or diagonally against the trellis and one vertically. Repeat until the desired height is reached. The leader can then be pruned.

The **palmette verrier**, named for Louis Verrier, a 19th-century French horticulturist, is a candelabra-like variation on the horizontal T or palmette oblique. As with those patterns, whips should be planted at least 8 feet apart and trimmed where they meet the lowest wire in a framework or the bottom of the trellis. Select the three best shoots that appear and remove the others. As the shoots grow, train two to the horizontal wires or to the trellis and let the central one grow vertically. When the side branches are 2 to 3 feet long, gradually bend them upward to 90 degrees, making the "candelabra" shape, tying the branches to diagonal stakes attached to the wires, or to the trellis.

If the branches are stiff and resist bending, use an ordinary carpenter's saw to make fine cuts halfway through them, 1 or 2 inches apart, on the outside of the bend. This allows a sharper angle to be made. The cuts will heal nicely. Early the next spring, cut the leader at the second wire, select the three best shoots that appear below the cut and train two horizontally and one vertically. Bend the horizontal shoots as above. If you like, repeat the process for two more years to make a 4-tier palmette verrier.

SEVERAL TRADITIONAL VARIATIONS of U-shapes, sometimes called candelabras, such as a single U, a double U and a triple U, can be accomplished by using techniques similar to that involved in the palmette verrier. Like the palmette verrier, they are grown from a single trunk and branch into upward-pointing U's. U-shapes, however, do not branch from a central stem. To form a single U-shape, plant a whip and cut it off at the first wire or the bottom of the trellis. Prune away all but two shoots that grow under the cut, training them horizontally along the lowest wire or portion of the trellis. When the shoots have grown at least 1 to 2 feet apart, gradually bend the tips upward, tying them to the trellis with stakes to bridge any gaps, or using stakes tied securely to the wires, until the two branches form a U-shape. For a double U, proceed for the first growing season as for a single U. The following spring, cut the two branches at the second wire, or 12 to 18 inches above the first cut the year before. Train the two strongest shoots on each branch horizontally, and sweep the tips up gradually to form two Us. For a triple U, plant and cut the whip as for a single U, but save the three best shoots. Train two shoots horizontally and one vertically, and

Apple blossoms on this espalier, a palmette verrier, demonstrate graphically the location of spurs. These short, thick twigs are the site of all flowering and fruit production, and should not be pruned.

sweep the tips of the outer ones upward. The following season, cut all three branches at the second wire or 12 to 18 inches above the cut the year before. Save the two best shoots that appear on each branch and train them horizontally, sweeping the tips upward to make three U-shapes.

Some think that the **Belgian fence** and **losange**, which form diagonal latticework patterns, are the most striking espaliers. Like other espaliers, they are handsome even when the plants are bare, but many find that the lattice effect of these two patterns is especially compelling. The Belgian fence and losange were

devised specifically for apples and pears, though other species can be adapted. Traditionally, plants in these espaliers are trained at a 45-degree angle, but an angle of 60 degrees can also be used. Plant the whips normally, and when they approach the first wire, remove all but the best 2 shoots. Attach stakes to the wires or to the trellis at 45- or 60-degree angles and train the shoots along them, forming a Y. The plants will overlap one another, forming a delicate latticework. When the top of the wires or the trellis is reached, do not prune the leaders, but bend them horizontally and train them along the uppermost wire to give a finished edge. The losange variation extends selected side shoots from the main branches into the lattice pattern to yield an even denser, more decorative effect.

Early production of fruit is the main advantage of the **Drapeau Marchand** espalier, which originated in France and is used by commercial orchards. Drapeau Marchand can be applied to apples and pears, as well as peaches, nectarines and apricots. Plant the trees about 6 to 8 feet apart, positioning them in the ground so that the trunks are at a 40-to-60-degree angle. To help the stems to stay at that angle, tie them to stakes that have been securely tied to the wires or trellis. Every foot or so, select shoots growing at a 90-degree angle from the slant of the stems and tie them to stakes fixed at that angle or to the trellis, using stakes to bridge any gaps. As the stems and branches grow, prune to maintain them at a manageable height. When the leader reaches the top of the support structure, remove any stakes and tie the stems loosely to the wires or trellis.

For the **arcure** form of espalier, select whips that are 3 to 4 feet tall and plant them at a slight angle 2 or 3 feet apart. Do not cut them off at 12 inches. After new growth has begun, bend all the whips in the same direction and tie them to the first wire or to the trellis in arches. Prune all shoots but one at the top center of each arch. As the top center shoots grow, bend them down into arches in the opposite direction and tie them in place to the second wire, or 12 to 18 inches above the first arches. Prune any shoots on these new branches except for one in the top center of each branch. As they grow, bend the shoots down into arches in the same direction as the first arch, and tie them to the third wire, or 12 to 18 inches above the second arches. Repeat, creating an alternately arching pattern, until the top of the trellis, wall or framework is reached.

For a **braided** espalier, plant two whips 6 inches to 1 foot apart and gradually bend their stems away from each other to the horizontal, training them along the lowest wire in the framework or low on the trellis. Allow one shoot to develop near the top of each bend, pruning all others. Train the shoots towards each other, overlapping them and tying them to the next wire up or to the trellis about 12 to 18 inches above the first arch. The first part of the braid is now formed. As before, train the branches to the horizontal wire or horizontally on the trellis, and prune all shoots, allowing only one to develop near the top of the bend on each second branch. Again, bend these shoots towards each other, overlapping them and tying them to the trellis or the next wire up, then training them to the horizontal. Continue the process until the top of the wire or the trellis is reached.

An almost unlimited number of patterns can be created with an informal or free-form espalier. One way to begin is to select a young plant that already has an interesting trunk or branch structure and capitalize on it by removing any branches or shoots that are not in keeping with the design. The best shape for stone fruits such as peaches, nectarines and apricots, as well as many ornamental species such as roses and forsythia, is a simple fan. A **fan-shaped** espalier may have one or more stems rising from the ground in any picturesque fashion that appeals to you.

To make a single-stemmed **fan**, plant an unbranched whip, cutting above at least four closely spaced buds. Save the four best shoots that appear, tying them to stakes attached to wires or to the trellis, the top two at an angle of 45 degrees and the bottom two at 30 degrees. The following spring, cut all four branches back, saving the six best shoots that develop. Train them to stakes spaced at even intervals to form a fan shape. During the third growing season, you may permit more shoots to develop on secondary branches, expanding the fan shape, or you may choose to allow the existing branches to elongate until the top and edge of the support is reached.

Small, informally espaliered shrubs break up the outline of this fence, softening its visual impact.

SELECTED SPECIES FOR ESPALIERS

Note: Heights are given for unespaliered plants. The height of an espaliered plant, controlled by bending and pruning, will often be considerably less.

FRUITS

Malus pumila
(apple)
Formal espalier (all forms).
Height: dwarfs to 8 feet, semi-dwarfs to 15 feet.
Sun.
Well-drained, slightly acid soil.
Zones 4-8.
Features: These familiar fruits are grown in countless varieties and do well in all forms of espaliers. Use dwarf or semidwarf trees. Dwarfs will bear fruit two or three years after planting, semidwarfs in three or four years. The fragrant 1-to-1½-inch blossoms change from pink to white as they open in the spring.
Varieties: Check with your local nursery as to the varieties best suited for your area. Good varieties for the coldest regions (Zone 4) are 'Anoka' and 'Wealthy', whose fruits mature in early fall, and 'Harlson' and 'Secor', late fall. Dependable in the East in Zones 5-7 are 'Early McIntosh', 'Gravenstein' and 'Lodi', early summer; 'Cortland', 'Macoun', 'McIntosh' and 'Red Delicious', late summer; and 'Jonathan', 'Golden Delicious', 'Grimes Golden' and 'Northern Spy', late fall. Varieties recommended for the Northwest in Zones 5-7 are 'Gravenstein' and 'Lodi', early summer; 'Starkrimson' and 'Starkspur', late summer; and 'Golden Delicious', 'Jonathan' and 'Rome Beauty', late fall. In northern California in Zones 5-7, good choices are 'Red June', early summer; 'Gravenstein', midsummer;

Malus pumila **(apple),** *above and left*

'Jonathan', early fall; 'Golden Delicious', fall; 'Rome Beauty', late fall. If you live in the southern edge of the apple-growing area (Zone 8), try 'Summer Champion', late summer; 'Winter Banana', fall; and 'Tropical Beauty', late fall.
Planting and care: For proper cross-pollination, plant trees of two varieties that bloom together within 50 feet of one another.

Plant in early spring in Zones 4 and 5, in fall in Zones 6-8. Keep the knobby bud union of dwarfed trees at least 2 inches above the soil. After some fruit has fallen naturally in early summer, thin the remaining fruit so that the apples are 6 to 7 inches apart. Apple trees produce fruit on spurs, small, contorted shoots less than 6 inches long with swollen, roundish buds surrounded by clusters of leaves. Do not prune after September 1, or you will encourage tender growth that could be killed by frost. Consult your county extension agent for a spraying schedule to ensure pest-free fruit. Pick apples by raising the fruit to one side and twisting; do not yank it off, or you may damage the spur on which future fruit will be borne.

Prunus armeniaca
(apricot)
Formal espalier (cordon, fan or Belgian fence).
Height: dwarf varieties to 8 feet.
Sun.
Slightly alkaline soil.
Zones 4-8.
Features: Apricots have attractive pink flowers that open in early spring—so early that they are sometimes nipped by frosts. The

blossoms are followed in late summer by 1½-inch fruits that have sweet orange flesh.

Varieties: 'Moorpark' and 'Early Golden' are varieties adaptable to many zones. Favorite varieties in California are 'Blenheim', 'Royal'

***Prunus armeniaca* (apricot)**

and 'Tilton'. In Zone 4, 'Moongold' and 'Sungold' are recommended (unlike most apricots, which bear fruit when planted alone, these two must be planted together to ensure cross-pollination).

Planting and care: Plant in spring in Zones 4 and 5 as early as the ground can be worked, in fall in Zones 6-8. Keep the knobby bud union of dwarfed trees at least 2 inches above the soil. Do not plant in pockets of low terrain susceptible to frost. If the leaf color becomes pale or yellowish, feed the trees in early spring with a scattering of 10-10-10 fertilizer scratched into the ground. Apricots bear fruit on

stems formed during the previous year. For a continual supply of new wood, prune each new shoot back to two buds in summer when the shoots are about a foot long, producing two new shoots; the following year, one of these shoots should be allowed to bloom and bear fruit while the other is again pruned back to two buds. When the fruits become about ¾ inch in diameter, thin them so that the remaining fruits are about 3 inches apart. Consult your county extension agent for a spraying schedule to ensure pest-free fruit.

Prunus avium (sweet cherry); *Prunus cerasus* (sour cherry)

Formal espalier (cordon, fan or Belgian fence).
Height: dwarfs to 20 feet.
Sun.
Well-drained, alkaline soil.
Zones 4-7.

Features: Sweet cherries bear 1-inch white blossoms and red, black or yellow 1-inch fruits that can be eaten either raw or cooked. Unless restrained by espaliering, standard trees grow to 25 feet tall with an equal spread; dwarf varieties grow lower. Sour cherries have 1-inch white blossoms and ¾-inch red or yellow fruits that are most frequently used in cooking and canning; they grow about 6 to 15 feet tall.

Varieties: Two of the best sweet cherries for cold areas are 'Lambert' and 'Windsor'. In the East,

recommended varieties are 'Black Tartarian', 'Napoleon', 'Windsor' and 'Emperor Francis'; in the West, good choices are 'Bing', 'Black Tartarian', 'Lambert', 'Napoleon', 'Van' and 'Vista'. A particularly good sour cherry tree is 'Montmorency', which grows to 15 feet tall; 'Meteor' reaches 12 feet and 'North Star' 8 feet.

Planting and care: Plant in early spring in Zones 4 and 5, in fall in Zones 6 and 7. Set out two varieties of sweet cherries to ensure proper cross-pollination; sour cherries are self-fertile. Prune to remove dead or diseased branches, and any that do not contribute to your espalier design. If foliage turns pale or yellowish, scatter a little 10-10-10 fertilizer beneath the plants and scratch it into the soil. Birds relish cherries and eat them as soon as they begin to show a tinge of ripe color; to protect them, cover the espaliers with plastic garden netting (or plant a mulberry tree nearby as a diversionary tactic—birds love mulberries even more). Cherries keep best if picked with the stems attached; grasp the stems and twist them, taking care not to break off the tiny spurs, on which fruit is borne.

Prunus persica (peach and nectarine)

Formal espalier (single U-shape, fan or Belgian fence).
Height: standard to 15 feet, dwarf 4 to 7 feet.
Sun.

Prunus persica (peach)

Well-drained, slightly acid soil. Zones 5-9.

Features: Peaches are fuzzy-skinned, nectarines are smooth-skinned; otherwise, they are essentially the same fruit. They are fairly easy to grow around much of the country, and a two-year-old tree will bear fruit within two or three years. Both are available as standard trees, which can be kept to 7 to 10 feet by espaliering, or smaller dwarfs. Flowers, ranging from pale pink to dark red, bloom before the leaves appear in spring. Fruits ripen in midsummer.

Varieties: Good peach varieties for cooler regions (Zones 5-8) are 'Harbelle', 'Reliance' and 'Sunapee'; those suited to Zones 6-8 are 'Halehaven', 'Redhaven' and 'Redskin'. Recommended for Zones 7-9 are 'Earligold', 'June Gold', 'Sam Houston' and 'Southland'. For Zone 9, try 'Early American' or 'Flordasun'. Nectarines that can be grown in

Zones 6-8 include 'Cavalier', 'Freedom', 'Nectarheart', 'Redbud' and 'Red Chief; in Zone 9, 'Sunred'.

Planting and care: Plant in early spring, on an elevated or sloping site if possible to prevent flower buds from being killed by spring frosts. For proper cross-pollination, trees of two varieties should be planted within 50 feet of one another. The first spring, dust 1 pound of 10-10-10 fertilizer around each tree, repeating the feeding about six weeks later. Peaches and nectarines bear fruit on branches that grew the previous year; old branches will not bear and should be cut away and replaced with new growth. To ensure a continual supply of new wood, prune each new shoot back to two buds in summer when the shoots are about a foot long, producing two new shoots. The following year, one of these shoots should be allowed to bloom and bear fruit while the other is again pruned back to two buds. Thin fruit to 6 to 8 inches apart on the branches. Pick the fruits in midsummer when they can be separated from the tree with little effort. Consult your county extension agent for a spraying schedule to ensure pest-free fruit.

Pyrus spp.
(pear)
Formal espalier (all forms).
Height: standard to 18 feet, dwarf to 10 feet.
Sun.
Heavy, moist but well-drained,

slightly acid soil.
Zones 5-9.

Features: In the spring, pear trees are covered with lovely white blossoms, followed in the summer and fall by delicious fruits, which are yellow, red or brown. Dwarf trees one or two years old will often fruit the second or third year. They are extremely long-lived, often bearing fruit for one hundred years.

Varieties: Consult a local nursery for pear varieties suited to your area. Among the many that grow well from coast to coast in Zones 5-7 is the early-ripening 'Clapp's Favorite'. Midseason varieties include 'Bartlett', 'Bosc',

Pyrus 'Bartlett' (Bartlett pears)

'Duchess', 'Magness', 'Orient' (Zones 5-9), 'Seckel', 'Starking Delicious' and 'Tyson' (all Zones 5-8). Late-ripeners include 'Anjou', 'Comice' (Zones 5-8), 'Kieffer' (Zones 4-9), 'LeConte' (Zones 5-9) and 'Moonglow' (Zones 5-8).

Planting and care: Plant in spring, or in fall in the South. For proper cross-pollination, set out trees of two different varieties that bloom together ('Duchess' is self-pollinating and can be planted alone). Some of the young fruit will drop about six weeks after the flowers bloom; thin out the remaining fruit so that the pears are about 6 to 8 inches apart. Do not allow fruit to ripen on the tree; harvest pears when they have reached full size but are still green and firm

(pears, like apples, bear fruit on spurs, which should not be damaged during picking). Keep the fruit in a cool, dark place to ripen. If fireblight is detected—a symptom is new spring growth wilting and turning black—cut off any blighted shoots several inches below the infection, wiping pruning tools with rubbing alcohol or a 10 percent bleach solution after each cut. Consult your county extension agent for a spraying schedule to ensure pest-free fruit.

ORNAMENTALS

Acer palmatum 'Atropurpureum'
(bloodleaved or red Japanese maple)
Informal espalier.
Height to 20 feet.
Partial shade.
Moist, well-drained soil.
Zones 5-8.
Features: A small deciduous tree with sharply cut leaves, purplish red all season, that provides a striking silhouette. Low side

---

Acer palmatum 'Atropurpureum' (red Japanese maple)

branches give a multiple-stemmed effect.

Varieties: *A. palmatum* has plain green leaves. *A. palmatum* 'Dissectum' (threadleaved Japanese maple), a very slow-growing variety whose even more finely divided leaves remain dark red all season, has pendulous branches that sometimes cascade to the ground; it can be grown as an espalier 4 to 8 feet high.

Planting and care: Plant in spring in soil well supplemented with peat moss or leaf mold. Trees do best in light, open shade. They grow at a slow rate and need little pruning.

Camellia japonica
(common camellia)
Formal or informal espalier.
Height 10 feet or more.
Partial shade.
Light, acid, moist soil.
Zones 7-10.

Features: In warmer climates, evergreen camellias make spectacular espaliers. They offer a wide variety of choices, with their dark, glossy, leathery leaves and single, semidouble or double flowers in many colors appearing in fall, winter and early spring. There are also many varieties of *C. sasanqua* (sansanqua camellia), which will grow as far north as Zone 7.

Varieties: Among the cultivars that do well as espaliers are 'Bride's Bouquet', 'Elegans', 'French Imperator', 'Lady Clare', 'Masterpiece' and 'Ville de

Nantes'.

Planting and care: Plant in spring in the northern edge of the plants' range, any time from fall through spring farther south. Set plants 1 inch higher in the

Camellia japonica
(common camellia)

soil than they had been growing at the nursery. Do not cultivate the soil for fear of damaging the shallow roots; instead, mulch the ground with a 2-to-3-inch layer of pine needles or ground bark. Prune immediately after flowering.

Cedrus atlantica glauca
(blue Atlas cedar)
Formal or informal espalier.
Height to 30 feet or more.
Sun.
Well-drained soil.
Zones 6-8.

Features: A distinctive, somewhat sparse evergreen whose whorls of pale blue-green needles grow on short spurs. The 3-inch cones are borne upright.

Varieties: *C. atlantica glauca pendula*, the weeping blue Atlas cedar, has branches that cascade gracefully.

Planting and care: Plant container-grown plants at any time during the growing season, balled-and-burlapped trees in early or late summer. Prune in spring.

Cercis canadensis
(Eastern redbud)
Informal espalier.
Height to 30 feet.
Sun or light shade.
Moist, well-drained soil.
Zones 3-9.

Features: An attractive small deciduous tree. Its branches are covered in early spring with clusters of ½-inch purplish pink blossoms before the 3-to-5-inch glossy green leaves unfurl. Foliage turns yellow before dropping in fall.

Varieties: A delightful white-flowered variety is *C. canadensis* 'Alba'.

Planting and care: Prepare the soil deep enough to accommodate the tree's long roots. Balled-and-burlapped or container-grown plants should be set in the ground in spring in most areas except the warmest climates, where they can be planted at any time from fall through spring. Prune in late winter, before new growth begins.

Chaenomeles speciosa
(flowering quince)
Informal espalier.
Height 5 to 6 feet.

Sun.

Most soils.

Zones 4-10.

Features: Spectacular displays of early-spring flowers—white, pink, orange or red—are followed by shiny red leaves, which turn a deep green in summer.

Varieties: Cultivars include 'Nivalis' and 'Snow' (white flowers), 'Phyllis Moore' and 'Gaujardii' (deep pink), 'Apple Blossom' and 'Marmorata' (pink and white) and 'Cardinalis' (red). *C. sinensis* (Chinese quince) bears pale pink flowers in spring; its dark green, leathery leaves turn scarlet in autumn.

Planting and care: Because it begins growing so early in the spring, try to plant flowering quince in the fall, particularly if bought bare-rooted. Prune right after the flowers have faded.

Cotoneaster spp.

(cotoneaster)

Informal espalier.

Height to 5 feet.

Sun.

Well-drained soil.

Zones 5-10.

Features: Cotoneasters have branches in flat sprays that espalier well. They are grown less for their small flowers than for their berries, which turn red in early fall, and their bright red-orange fall foliage.

Varieties: *C. divaricatus* (spreading cotoneaster) bears inconspicuous pink flowers in spring, followed by handsome red berries. *C. franchetii* (Franchet cotoneaster) bears orange-red

berries.

Planting and care: Plant container-grown plants at any time during the growing season. Allow room for the plants to develop; the arching branches lose much of their beauty if clipped off. Prune in early spring before new growth begins.

Forsythia spp.

(forsythia)

Formal or informal espalier.

Height to 8 feet.

Sun or light shade.

Most soils.

Zones 5-9.

Features: The taller types of forsythia make good espaliers. *F. x intermedia* (border forsythia) bears large quantities of yellow 2-inch blossoms on upright stems in early spring. *F. suspensa* (weeping forsythia) has long, arching canes.

Varieties: Excellent cultivars of border forsythia include 'Spectabilis', 'Beatrix Farrand', 'Karl Sax' and 'Lynwood Gold'. A good choice among weeping forsythias is *F. suspensa* var. *fortunei*.

Planting and care: Plant in spring. Prune immediately after the flowers have faded.

Ilex spp.

(holly)

Formal or informal espalier.

Height to 10 feet.

Sun or partial shade.

Moist, slightly acid soil.

Zones 7-10.

Features: Of the many hollies, ranked among the most stunning

of broad-leaved evergreens, several can be espaliered with striking results.

Varieties: *I. cornuta* 'Burfordii' (Burford Chinese holly) bears dark green, spineless and glossy leaves up to 4 inches long, and large orange-red berries. *I. crenata* 'Convexa' (convexleaf Japanese holly) has dense, shiny ½-inch leaves.

Planting and care: Plant in spring, or in fall in the southern zones. Hollies will grow in light shade, but will bear fewer berries than they will in full sun; to assure berries, set out both male and female plants. Do not cultivate, but instead mulch with a 2-to-3-inch layer of pine needles, wood chips or ground bark. In the northern part of their range, give plants winter shade and protection from wind. Prune in early spring before new growth begins, working in a dusting of cottonseed meal or acid fertilizer at the same time.

Jasminium nudiflorum

(winter jasmine)

Informal espalier.

Height to 15 feet.

Sun.

Well-drained soil.

Zones 6-9 (and sheltered spots in Zone 5).

Features: In early spring—in winter in the South—the long arching stems of winter jasmine are lined with bright yellow 1-inch flowers. The slender twigs make a delicate tracery against a wall.

Planting and care: Plant in

Pyracantha spp. (firethorn)

spring. If early blossoms are desired, set in a sunny place. Prune immediately after flowering.

Laburnum x *watereri*
(waterer goldenchain)
Formal or informal espalier.
Height to 20 feet.
Partial shade.
Moist, well-drained soil.
Zones 6-9.
Features: In midspring, this deciduous tree puts on a splendid display of bright yellow 1-inch flowers, which hang in clusters as long as 20 inches. Every part of the plant is poisonous.
Planting and care: Plant in spring, in soil deep enough to accommodate the long roots. Trees do best where they get light shade, especially during the hot part of the day, and should be sheltered from the wind. Since rabbits like to nibble at the bark, enclose the lower stems in the wire mesh called hardware cloth. Prune in early summer after flowering to remove seed pods and dead branches, and to stimulate the production of new flowering shoots for the following year.

Magnolia spp.
(magnolia)
Formal or informal espalier.
Height to 30 feet or more.
Sun or light shade.
Rich, moist, acid soil.
Zones 4-10.
Features: A classic espalier that can be held to 8 feet or less by pruning. Leaves are large, oval, dark green and glossy. Flowers

are large, white or pink and in some cases fragrant. Plants can be grown as espaliers north of prescribed zones if given shade and wind protection.

Varieties: *M. grandiflora* (Southern magnolia), whose white, fragrant flowers are up to 8 inches across appear in late May, makes an impressive espalier if a tall enough wall surface is available. *M.* x *soulangiana* (saucer magnolia), begins to blossom when it is about 4 feet tall, bears large white, pink to purplish flowers and is somewhat smaller than the Southern magnolia; its fruit looks like a knobby cucumber and when ripe opens to display bright red berries. *M. stellata* (star magnolia) is smaller still, beginning to flower when only 3 feet tall, bearing fragrant white flowers 3 inches across.

Planting and care: Plant in spring, making sure to set plants at the same height they were growing at the nursery. Choose a variety with widely spaced branches to ensure good flower production. Prune immediately after flowering.

Malus spp.
(crabapple)
Formal or informal espalier.
Height to 20 feet.
Sun.
Moist, well-drained, acid soil.
Zones 4-9.
Features: Among the easiest to grow and most resistant to cold of all flowering trees, crabapples are smothered in 1-to-2-inch apple-blossom-scented flowers in

spring, before the leaves unfurl. These are followed in summer by clusters of fruits, which can be left for the birds or made into a tasty jelly. Crabapples have oval 2-to-4-inch leaves with sawtooth edges.

Varieties: Of the many varieties of crabapple suitable for espaliering are *Malus* 'Dorothea', which bears enormous numbers of 1½-to-2-inch pink semidouble flowers in spring, followed in summer by ½-inch bright yellow fruits. Another is *M.* 'Red Jade', a handsome weeping variety that is covered with 1-inch white blossoms followed by bright red berries.

Planting and care: Plant in spring or early fall. Crabapples grow rapidly and start to flower at an early age. Prune trees in late winter or early spring, taking care to leave the short stubby spurs on which the blossoms and fruits will appear.

Prunus spp.
(flowering cherry)
Formal or informal espalier.
Height to 20 feet.
Sun.
Rich, moist soil.
Zones 5-9.
Features: Flowering cherries bear spectacular masses of 1-to-2-inch blossoms before or at the same time the leaves begin to unfold. The leaves are 3 to 5 inches long with serrated edges.
Varieties: *P. serrulata* 'Amanogawa' (Amanogawa flowering cherry, Oriental cherry) bursts into bloom in spring with 1¾-inch light pink, semidouble

flowers. *P. subhirtella* 'Pendula' (weeping Higan or rosebud cherry) bears cascades of 1-inch light pink, single flowers on gracefully drooping branches.
Planting and care: Plant in early spring. Prune immediately after flowering.

Pyracantha spp.
(firethorn)
Formal or informal espalier.
Height to 12 feet.
Sun or partial shade.
Well-drained soil.
Zones 4-9.
Features: White flowers in late spring are followed by bright masses of orange berries that often last into the winter. Plants have ½-inch thorns. Pyracantha is a species so often used as an espalier that some nurseries sell plants already trained into espalier form.
Varieties: The hardiest cultivar, able to withstand winters in Zone 4, is *P. angustifolia* Yukon Belle 'Monon', which forms up-

Taxus spp. (yew)

right branches 6 to 8 feet high. *P. coccinea* 'Kasan' (Zone 5) grows 8 to 10 feet tall, as does *P. koidzumii* 'Victory' (Zone 7) and *P. coccinea* 'Mohave' (Zone 6), which bears huge masses of berries early in the season. *P. fortuneana* 'Graberi' (Zone 7) grows vigorously to 10 or 12 feet.

Planting and care: Plant in early spring. Pyracantha is fast-growing, and can be trained to almost any pattern. To produce compact clusters of fall and winter berries, cut back new growth after the plant blooms to just above the first flower clusters.

Taxus spp.

(yew)
Formal or informal espalier.
Height to 15 feet.
Sun or shade.
Well-drained, slightly acid soil.
Zones 5-9.
Features: Among the most versatile of narrow-leaved evergreens

for home use, yews grow slowly when young; they are relatively expensive but are good investments over the long haul (some yew hedges in England are over 300 years old). Yews boast rich green, shiny needles about ¾ inch long that sprout featherlike along the branches. The red berries, bark and needles are poisonous.

Varieties: Among the yews suitable for espaliering are *T. baccata* 'Repandens' (spreading English yew), *T. cuspidata* 'Nana' (dwarf Japanese yew), *T. x media* 'Hicksii' (Hicks yew) and *T. x media* 'Wardii' (Ward's yew)

Planting and care: Plant in spring. To speed growth and maintain rich foliage color, feed once a year in spring with cottonseed meal or a balanced fertilizer such as 5-10-5. Yews cannot tolerate soil that stays wet and soggy. Prune early in the season, before new growth begins.

Viburnum spp.

(viburnum)
Formal or informal espalier.
Height to 20 feet.
Sun or partial shade.
Well-drained soil.
Zones 4-9.
Features: Viburnums are attractive shrubs that bear masses of round or flat-topped flower clusters in spring, followed by berries that eventually turn black in fall (those of black haw can be made into tasty jams or jellies). The foliage turns shades of red in fall.

Varieties: Good espaliers can be made of *V. plicatum* (Japanese snowball), *V. plicatum* var. *tomentosum* (doublefile viburnum), *V. prunifolium* (black haw) and *V. sieboldii* (Siebold viburnum).

Planting and care: Plant in spring. Container-grown plants can be set in the ground at any time from spring through early fall. Prune after flowering.

A LIST OF SPECIES BY FUNCTION

Espaliers for Edible Fruit

Malus pumila (apple)
Prunus armeniaca (apricot)
Prunus avium (sweet cherry)
Prunus cerasus (sour cherry)
Prunus persica (peach and nectarine)
Pyrus (pear)

Espaliers for Flowers

Camellia japonica

(common camellia)
Cercis canadensis
   (Eastern redbud)
Chaenomeles speciosa
   (flowering quince)
Forsythia spp. (forsythia)
Jasminium nudiflorum
   (winter jasmine)
Laburnum x *watereri*
   (waterer goldenchain)
Magnolia spp. (magnolia)
Malus spp. (crabapple)
Prunus spp. (flowering cherry)

Pyracantha spp. (firethorn)
Viburnum spp. (viburnum)

Espaliers for Foliage and Form

Acer palmatum 'Atropurpureum'
   (bloodleaved or red
   Japanese maple)
Cedrus atlantica glauca
   (blue Atlas cedar)
Cotoneaster spp. (cotoneaster)
Ilex spp. (holly)
Taxus spp. (yew)

SOURCES
PLANTS & SEED TO MAKE A LIVING FENCE

Vernon Barnes & Son Nursery
P. O. Box 250
McMinnville, TN 37110-0250
(615) 668-8576
Flowering trees, fruit trees, vines, etc. Free catalog.

Baycreek Gardens
P. O. Box 339
Grayson, GA 30221
(404) 339-1600
Conifers, shrubs, etc., especially for southern regions. Free catalog.

Burpee
300 Park Avenue
Warminster, PA 18974
(215) 674-4900
Trees, fruit trees, shrubs, vines. Free catalog.

Country Dell
9760 SE 302nd Lane, Div. M
Boring, OR 97009
(503) 663-6123
Ornamental shrubs. Free catalog.

DeGiorgi Seed Company
6011 'N' Street
Omaha, NE 68117-1634
(402) 731-3901
1500 seed varieties offered. Free catalog.

Dominion Seed House
Box 2500
Georgetown, Ontario
L7G 5L6
(905) 873-3037
Free catalog.

Farmer Seed & Nursery Co.
1706 Morrissey Drive
Bloomington, IL 61704
(309) 662-3511
Shrubs and trees shipped bare-root. Free catalog.

Henry Field's
415 N. Burnett St.
Shenandoah, IA 51602
(605) 665-4491
Ornamental and fruit trees, shrubs, hedges and vines. Free catalog.

Gardeners' Choice
County Road 687
Hartford, MI 49057
(800) 451-9001
Fruit trees, vines, shrubs. Free catalog.

Gurney's Seed & Nursery Co.
110 Capital Street
Yankton, SD 57079
(605) 665-1671
Trees, shrubs, fruit and berry hedges. Free catalog.

House of Wesley, Inc.
1704 Morrissey Drive
Bloomington, IL 61704
(309) 663-9551
Shrubs and trees shipped mostly bare-root. Free catalog.

Jackson & Perkins
1 Rose Lane
Medford, OR 97501
(800) 854-6200
New and award-winning J & P roses. Free catalog.

Jung Seed Company
335 S. High Street
Randolph, WI 53957-0001
(414) 326-3123
Heirloom seeds, landscape plants and fruit trees. Free catalog.

Kelly Nurseries
1706 Morrissey Drive
Bloomington, IL 61704
(309) 663-9551
Trees, ornamental plants, roses, fruit trees. Free catalog.

Henry Leuthardt
P. O. Box 666
East Moriches, NY 11940
(516) 878-1387
Specialist in espalier-trained fruit trees and grape vines. Free catalog.

McFayden
30 Ninth St.
Brandon, Manitoba
R7A YA4
(204) 725-7314
Largest mail order seed company in Canada. Fruit trees and ornamental shrubs. Free catalog.

Mellinger's
2310 W. South Range Road
North Lima, OH 44452-9731
(216) 549-9861
Seeds, plants, trees, including many rare and hard-to-find items. Free catalog.

Michigan Bulb Co.
1950 Waldorf NW
Grand Rapids, MI 49550
(616) 771-9500
Roses, trees and shrubs in addition to bulbs. Free catalog.

Miller Nurseries
5060 West Lake Road
Canandaigua, NY 14424
(800) 836-9630
Semi-dwarf and standard fruit trees, flowering trees and shrubs, roses. Free catalog.

Musser Forests, Inc.
P. O. Box 340
Dept. 18-94
Indiana, PA 15701-0340
(412) 465-5685
Northern-grown seedlings and transplants for hedges, windbreaks and ornamental shrubs. Free catalog.

Northwoods Retail Nursery
27635 S. Oglesby Road
Canby, OR 97013-9528
(503) 266-5432
Unique fruit and ornamental trees: apples, cherries, pears, peaches, nectarines. Free catalog.

Owen Farms
2951 Curve-Nankipoo Road
Route 3, Box 158A
Ripley, TN 38063-9420
(901) 635-1588
Trees, shrubs, etc. Catalog $2.00

Park Seed
P. O. Box 31, Highway 254
Greenwood, SC 29648-0031
(803) 223-8555
3,000 varieties of flower seeds and plants, including roses. Free catalog.

W. H. Perron
2914 Labelle Boulevard
(Chomedey)
Laval, Quebec H7P 5R9
(514) 332-3619
Fruit trees, roses, shrubs. Free catalog.

Raintree Nursery
391 M Butts Road
Morton, WA 98356-9700
(206) 496-6400
Specializing in apples, pears, peaches, bamboos, apricots. Free catalog.

Southmeadow Fruit Gardens
Box SM
Lakeside, MI 49116
(616) 469-2865
Unusual apples, grapes, pears, peaches, nectarines, plums, apricots, cherries. Catalog $9.00 prepaid. Price list free.

Spring Hill Nurseries
6523 North Galena Road
NA9948A4
Peoria, IL 61632
(309) 689-3828
Specializing in top quality roses, trees and shrubs. Free catalog.

Stark Brothers
P. O. Box 10, Dept. B216AN
Louisiana, MO 63353-0010
(800) 325-4180
Fruit trees, shrubs, roses, flowering trees. Free catalog.

Thompson & Morgan
220 Farraday Avenue
P. O. Box 1308
Dept. 104-4
Jackson, NJ 08527-0308
(908) 363-2225
Flower seeds and plants. Many rare items. Free catalog.

Wayside Gardens
1 Garden Lane
Hodges, SC 29695-0001
(803) 223-7333
Ornamental shrubs and trees. Free catalog.

White Flower Farm
Dept. 40910
Litchfield, CT 06759-0050
(203) 496-9600
Ornamental shrubs. Free catalog.

Winterthur
100 Enterprise Place, P-99.
Dover, DE 19901
(800) 767-0500
Unusual trees and shrubs, many exclusive to Winterthur. Free catalog.

FOR FURTHER READING

American Horticultural Society Illustrated Encyclopedia of Gardening. *Shrubs and Hedges.* Mt. Vernon, VA: American Horticultural Society, 1982.

Chamberlin, Susan. *Hedges, Screens and Espaliers: How to Select, Grow and Enjoy.* Tucson, AZ: HP Books, 1983.

Cox, Jeff. *From Vines to Wines.* New York: Harper & Row Publishers, 1985.

Cravens, Richard H. *Vines.* The Time-Life Encyclopedia of Gardening. New York: Time-Life Books, 1979.

Crockett, James Underwood. *Flowering Shrubs.* The Time-Life Encyclopedia of Gardening. New York: Time-Life Books, 1972.

Crockett, James Underwood. *Trees.* The Time-Life Encyclopedia of Gardening. New York: Time-Life Books, 1972.

Crockett, James Underwood. *Evergreens.* The Time-Life Encyclopedia of Gardening. New York: Time-Life Books, 1971.

Cutler, Karan Davis, ed. *Vines.* A Harrowsmith Gardener's Guide. Charlotte, VT: Camden House Publishing, Inc., 1992.

Gallup, Barbara and Deborah Reich. *The Complete Book of Topiary* (includes a chapter on espaliers). New York: Workman Publishing, 1987.

Hart, Rhonda Massingham. *Trellising: How to Grow Climbing Vegetables, Fruits, Flowers, Vines & Trees.* Pownal, VT: Storey Communications, Inc., 1992.

Howard, Frances. *Landscaping with Vines.* New York: The MacMillan Co., 1959.

Perkins, Harold O. *Espaliers and Vines for the Home Gardener.* Princeton, NJ: D. Van Nostrand Co., 1964.

Editors of Sunset magazine. *Landscaping for Privacy: Hedges, Fences, Arbors.* Menlo Park, CA: Lane Publishing Co., 1985.

Whitehead, Jeffrey. *The Hedge Book: How to Select, Plant and Grow a Living Fence.* Pownal, VT: Storey Communications, Inc., 1991.

Wyman, Donald. *Shrubs and Vines for American Gardens.* New York: MacMillan Publishing Co., 1969.

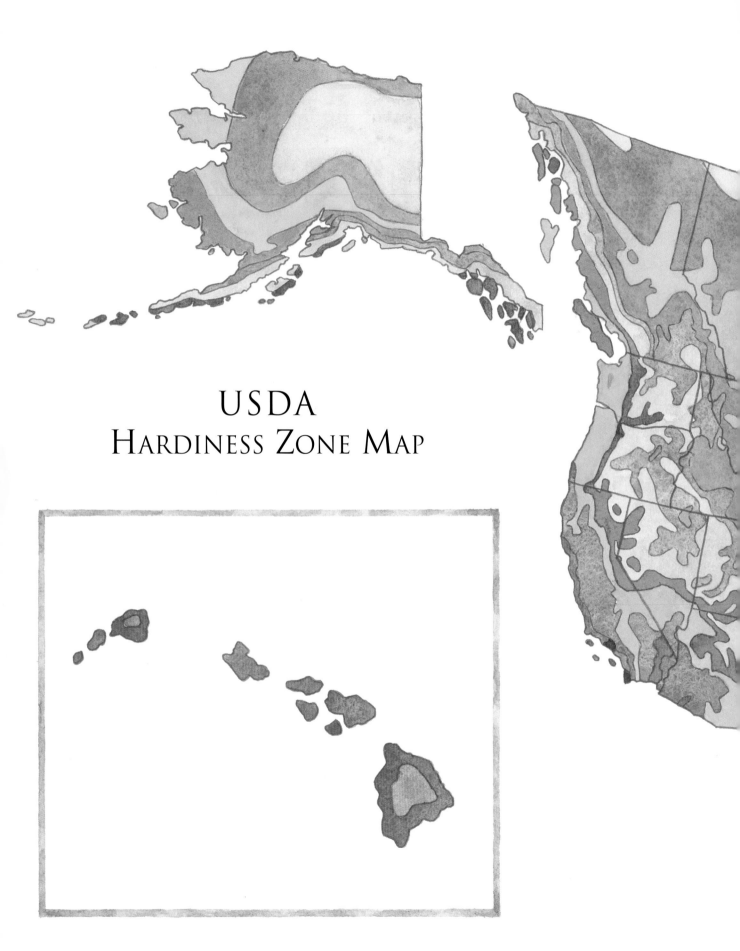

USDA
HARDINESS ZONE MAP

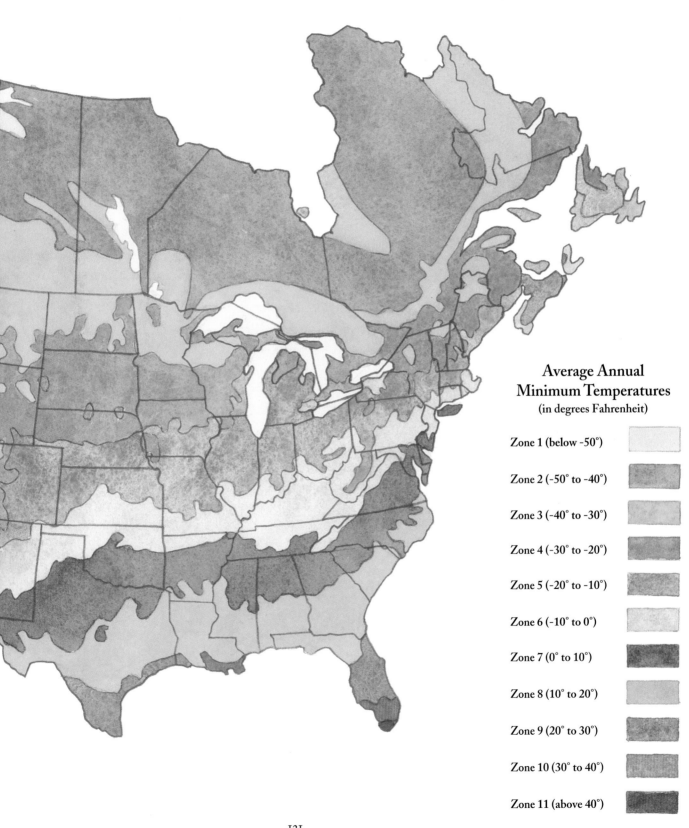

Average Annual
Minimum Temperatures
(in degrees Fahrenheit)

Zone 1 (below -50°)

Zone 2 (-50° to -40°)

Zone 3 (-40° to -30°)

Zone 4 (-30° to -20°)

Zone 5 (-20° to -10°)

Zone 6 (-10° to 0°)

Zone 7 (0° to 10°)

Zone 8 (10° to 20°)

Zone 9 (20° to 30°)

Zone 10 (30° to 40°)

Zone 11 (above 40°)

CREDITS

PHOTOGRAPHY

Richard Brown
Front cover; pages 14-15, 26-27, 28, 54 (bottom right), 55, 59, 65, 69, 70, 85, 86, 89, 93, 95, 103, 105, 114; back cover (top and bottom right)

Karen Bussolini
pages 92, 96, 106, 109 (bottom right), 113

Bruce Coleman Inc.
page 39, Jane Burton; 58, E. R. Degginger; 71, James H. Carmichael
74, Hans Reinhard; 84, Jack Dermid; 110, Norman Owen Tomalin
111, S. L. Craig

Derek Fell
pages 16, 30, 32, 33, 35, 37, 49, 50, 52, 53, 72 (top left and bottom right), 73, 75, 77, 78, 82, 88, 90-91, 107, 108, 109 (top left)

Grant Heilman Photography Inc.
page 9, Lefever/Grushow; 12, Jim Strawser; 13, Larry Lefever
29, Grant Heilman; 34, Lefever/Grushow; 38, Larry Lefever
40, Jane Grushow; 41, Larry Lefever; 42, Lefever/Grushow
44, Lefever/Grushow; 46, Jim Strawser; 47, Jim Strawser; 48, Grant Heilman
51, Lefever/Grushow; 54 (top, left) Larry Lefever; 60, Thomas Hovland
61, Jim Strawser; 62-63, Levefer/Grushow; 64, Lefever/Grushow
76, Larry Lefever; 79, Larry Lefever; 80, Lefever/Grushow
81, Lefever/Grushow; back cover (bottom right), Larry Lefever

ILLUSTRATIONS

Vince Babak
pages 17, 19, 21, 22, 24, 25, 66, 67, 94, 98, 100

Jean Carlson Masseau
USDA Zone Map, pages 120-121

INDEX